ON THE WAY

ON THE WAY

A GUIDE TO CHRISTIAN SPIRITUALITY

GORDON T. SMITH

NAVPRESS

Bringing Truth to Life
P.O. Box 35001, Colorado Springs, Colorado 80935

OUR GUARANTEE TO YOU

We believe so strongly in the message of our books that we are making this quality guarantee to you. If for any reason you are disappointed with the content of this book, return the title page to us with your name and address and we will refund to you the list price of the book. To help us serve you better, please briefly describe why you were disappointed. Mail your refund request to: NavPress, P.O. Box 35002, Colorado Springs, CO 80935.

The Navigators is an international Christian organization. Our mission is to reach, disciple, and equip people to know Christ and to make Him known through successive generations. We envision multitudes of diverse people in the United States and every other nation who have a passionate love for Christ, live a lifestyle of sharing Christ's love, and multiply spiritual laborers among those without Christ.

NavPress is the publishing ministry of The Navigators. NavPress publications help believers learn biblical truth and apply what they learn to their lives and ministries. Our mission is to stimulate spiritual formation among our readers.

Library of Congress Catalog Card Number: 2001032706
ISBN 1-57683-237-6

Cover design by David Carlson Design
Cover photo by Jules Frazier/PhotoDisc
Creative Team: Don Simpson, Amy Spencer, Glynese Northam

Some of the anecdotal illustrations in this book are true to life and are included with the permission of the persons involved. All other illustrations are composites of real situations, and any resemblance to people living or dead is coincidental.

Unless otherwise identified, all Scripture quotations in this publication are taken from the *New Revised Standard Version* (NRSV), copyright © 1989, by the Division of Christian Education of the National Council of the Churches of Christ in the USA, used by permission, all rights reserved. Other versions used include *The Holy Bible: New International Version* ® (NIV®). Copyright © 1973, 1978, 1984 by International Bible Society. Used by permission of Zondervan Publishing House. All rights reserved; and the *King James Version* (KJV).

Smith, Gordon T., 1953-
    On the way : a guide to Christian spirituality / Gordon T. Smith
    p.cm.
    Includes bibliographical references.
    ISBN 1-56783-237-6
    1. Spiritual life--Christianity. I. Title
BV4501.3 .S65 2001
248.4--dc21   2001032706

FOR A FREE CATALOG OF
NAVPRESS BOOKS & BIBLE STUDIES,
CALL 1-800-366-7788 (USA)
OR 1-416-499-4615 (CANADA)

Printed in the United States of America
1 2 3 4 5 6 7 8 9 10 / 05 04 03 02 01

To my parents,

◆ ◆ ◆ ◆ *Cecil and Eunice Smith*

◆ ◆ ◆ ◆ CONTENTS

◆ ◆ ◆ ◆ INTRODUCTION

Great athletes have mastered the fundamentals of their sport. What is amazing is the simple reality that they come back to these basic elements of their game again and again and again. When a baseball team gathers for spring training, both the veterans and the rookies start the new season by practicing the fundamentals of the game, the elemental skills that are critical to the team's success.

Similarly, renewal in the Christian life is consistently found in returning to the fundamentals: What does it mean to be a Christian? What is Christian spirituality? What are the essential elements of a dynamic faith? Renewal in the Christian life is not usually found in some new technique or method but in getting back to basics. What follows is meant to be precisely that: a guide for maturing Christians who need some coaching in this return to spiritual fundamentals.

A basic guide to the Christian life will enable us to live truthfully in an often perplexing and discouraging world. In chapter 17 of the gospel of John, Jesus is praying to the Father and in the prayer identifies two basic contours for the Christian life. His prayer affirms that His disciples are called to be in the world. In other words, the Christian identity is not one of disengagement from our world. However, Jesus also affirms that these same disciples do not belong to the world. This reality that they do not belong is captured by the word "sanctified" (verses 17-19). They are sanctified by the truth, and thus though they are *in* the

9

world, they are not *of* the world. In other words, we are called to be present to this world, to be men and women who are fully engaged with our culture and society. But though we are in the world, we are not of that world. Our values and worldview are fundamentally and radically different. We see differently, think differently, respond differently. And Jesus links this directly with joy. He has come that His disciples' joy would be made complete (John 16:24); and they will, it would seem, only know this complete joy insofar as they embrace the call to be in but not of the world.

Joy, then, is not found in disengagement from the world; joy is not found in isolation. Rather, we are people of joy when we learn how to be genuinely engaged with our world—but only, of course, if we are not *of* the world. This is a challenge. It takes so little for Christians to be blindsided, consumed by our cultural context, and unaware often of how we are overly identified with its longings, values, and aspirations. In order to be entirely engaged in our world yet not live by its values, our only recourse is to live in the reign of Jesus. We choose to live under Christ's kingdom authority, and we do so with a confidence that Jesus is the only hope we have for our tomorrow. If we are going to manage this, we need the wealth of wisdom from the Christian heritage that would enable us to understand and live with this dual identity of being in but not of the world.

Further, we want to be content in our Christian lives with nothing less than all that we are called to be. God's grace is sufficient, but we need to *appropriate* this grace. This requires that we be intentional and thoughtful, that we consider and act in a manner that is purposeful and disciplined.

We also need a *model* of the Christian life that encompasses the whole of our lives, not merely those elements that we normally think of as religious activities. We are called to live passionately and thoroughly—in every aspect of life and work—as women and men who love God and seek to serve Him in the church and in the world. And what we long for is an approach to the Christian life that will involve every aspect of our lives, from prayer to work, from the pattern of our relationships to our experience of recreation.

This book responds to such a need by pointing to the classic disciplines and components of a Christian spirituality that have been consistently affirmed by each generation of Christians. We have much to learn from the saints that have preceded us, and the chapters that follow seek to bring together some of the accumulated wisdom of our spiritual forefathers and mothers. And they will consistently call us to an appreciation of a profound reality: all that we are and hope to be is a gift from God. If we are going to live in but not of the world, it will be by the grace of God. What we seek, then, are practices and habits of the Christian life that enable us to experience this grace that empowers us to fulfill the call to follow Jesus. And this grace is a gift.

Jesus once identified this gift as "living water" (John 4:10,13). This living water has a property remarkably similar to the water we drink daily: it needs a container. Just as we cannot drink water unless it is contained in a pitcher or cup, so the living water of Jesus needs the container of spiritual discipline.

It's true that we must maintain a clear distinction between new life in Christ and spiritual discipline. The Christian life is the living water—a living personal relationship with God. The spiritual disciplines do not themselves constitute the Christian life. They belong with the Christian life, but they are not synonymous with the Christian life. Just as it is possible to have a pitcher and no refreshing water, it is possible to have spiritual disciplines and little, if any, authentic relationship with God.

Still, just as we cannot contain water without a pitcher or cup, so we need the disciplines to sustain and deepen the Christian life.

Sometimes these disciplines may seem too difficult, too hard or rigid. But there is a helpful way to think about this: when we drink cool, refreshing water from a cup, we certainly do not object that the cup from which we drink is hard and inflexible. We are thirsty, and the container allows us to drink freely. Similarly, we would be too hasty to protest that the spiritual disciplines of the Christian life seem hard or inflexible. With practice, we find that they are the precious channels of the living water we seek. They are not ends in themselves, but without them there is no living water.

We seek the living water without which we cannot live. A spirituality is a means to this end. It is a personalized pattern of integrated spiritual disciplines and intentional practices designed to enable us to grow in grace toward spiritual maturity. This pattern of disciplines and practices is not an end in itself; it is rather the means by which we experience the living water. However, what we need is not a one-size-fits-all spirituality. Rather, what we each need is a way, a path that fits us at this stage of life and that is congruent with the circumstances, challenges, and particularities of our lives. We seek living water and we will only know this gift when we return to the fundamental disciplines and practices of a true Christian spirituality. However, we return to the basics—the fundamentals of the spiritual life—to explore how these crucial elements can take shape in a way that fits us and enables us to grow in faith, hope, and love.

CHAPTER

◆ ◆ ◆ ◆ 1

A SPIRITUALITY THAT FITS

The hope and aim of the spiritual life is genuine and thorough spiritual transformation. God calls us to Himself and grants us His redemption, all with a driving and powerful resolution — that God would make us a new people that reflects His righteousness, His perfect and holy character. Any spiritual tradition that downplays the biblical call to personal and corporate holiness is not faithful to the biblical message. Holiness is not optional for someone who claims to be a child of God. If a spirituality fits us, the evidence of this is that we have a transforming relationship with God, a relationship that enables us to grow and mature in faith, hope, and love.

To know this transformation we must necessarily come to the disciplines and practices of the spiritual life with a resolve that we will turn from sin, long for the righteousness of God, and allow His Spirit to transform us into His image. In the biblical understanding, sin is not arbitrary or unrelated to life. Sin is death; it violates and undermines life and all that is important to life. If God longs for us to be freed from sin, it is for one reason: He longs for us to live. Sin is death; righteousness is life. Toleration of sin in our lives is as incongruous as a doctor remaining passive in the face of sickness. It is rejection of life and of God. This is the most helpful way to think about the biblical idea of holiness — as the full expression of health and life.

LONGING FOR TRANSFORMATION

It will take a long time before I forget my first two years in the Philippines. When my family moved there, we were involved in language study at first. Then I became an instructor in theology at a seminary in Manila. But what was most noteworthy in those initial years was that we became well acquainted with the local hospitals for the simple reason that, on average, once a month a member of our family was admitted for some reason or another. One of my sons had a serious allergic reaction that made it very difficult for him to breathe, and regularly we would be awakened in the night, alarmed at his condition, and rushing off to the emergency room. My wife at one point suffered from hepatitis and then later the dreaded dengue fever. I had typhoid fever that left me in bed for several weeks and feeling constantly weak for longer yet.

I remember once sitting in the waiting room of one of the hospitals when my wife had hepatitis. As I sat there I was struck by a fundamental longing from the depth of my being for health and strength. I longed for it for myself; I longed for it for my family. Nothing else seemed to matter—it was the dominant, central concern of my life. I was weary of sickness, of being in the hospital, of having to listen to doctors, even though they were well intentioned, sincere, and desiring to be helpful.

When my wife was well and back at home, I recalled that feeling, that intense longing for physical health, and I came to see that in a similar way holiness is nothing more than thorough and radical *wholeness* wherein our *entire* beings are healthy, right, and true. I saw that if we had eyes to see and ears to hear we would recognize that we are sick and we would seek holiness because we long for health and life. We would see that sin is sickness and death; holiness is life. And it would be evident that we truly live to the degree that we seek and know the holiness of God. The desire we have for a vital spirituality is essentially a longing for God and for wholeness in God. The hunger for spiritual maturity is a longing for life.

The biblical ideal of holiness—the wholeness for which we long—is summarized in the Old and New Testaments as love of God and neighbor. And an authentic Christian spirituality will enable us to grow in holiness—in the capacity to love God as the source and meaning of all life—but also to grow in our capacity to love others even as we have been loved. The key word here is "grow." For the Scriptures consistently portray the Christian life as one of progression and development. In many respects the very purpose of Christian spirituality is to foster this growth.

There are many metaphors or pictures of the spiritual life in the Bible, and one of the most compelling of these is the comparison of our lives with growing persons. As human beings, we begin small, as infants, and then we grow up physically and emotionally and become adults. In the same way, the Bible suggests that in the Christian life we begin as infants, babes in Christ.

In Scripture, the clear expectation is that we would grow up in our salvation and mature in our faith. We are called and empowered by God's Spirit to move on toward spiritual maturity. If we are "on the way," it is a way that beckons us forward toward greater spiritual maturity and strength.

My wife and I were thrilled when our sons were born; we delighted in everything about them when they were tiny little boys. And as I look back I remember very fondly their preschool days, when they were ages three, four, and five. Yet, however wonderful they were at this age, we certainly did not want them to stay there. Our deep delight was actually in watching them grow and mature, seeing them learn how to walk, speak, play, and work. It would have been both abnormal and tragic if they had not grown up. They were infants, but their infancy was only a transition to something else.

Similarly, the Christian life has a beginning, and the Scriptures often compare this to infancy. When we become Christians or when we are young in our faith, we are likened to newborn babies (1 Peter 2:2). But then the very acknowledgment of this spiritual infancy serves as a call to "long for the pure, spiritual milk, so that you may grow into salvation." The spiritual life, then, is to be characterized by genuine and identifiable spiritual growth and development. In Hebrews 5:12-13 the author of the biblical text shows the contrast between the Christian who is an infant and the Christian who is mature in faith and practice. He expresses dismay that some have not grown; they are still infants when they should have shown evidence that they were skilled "in the word of righteousness," as the author puts it.

It is tragic, then, that so many Christian believers seemingly never mature in their faith, never become individuals of spiritual depth, wisdom, and discernment. And we should feel this tragedy as keenly as we would feel it if a person remained perpetually an infant, physically and emotionally. What is beautiful in a young child becomes distressing when we find it in one who is older.

Even though I look back fondly on their preschool years, I wonder if the most special moment I had as a father happened much more recently, when with my two sons I stood on the twelfth tee of a local golf course waiting for the foursome ahead of us to move on down the fairway so we could tee off. As I stood there with these young men—both of whom would no doubt drive the ball farther and more accurately than I would!—I reveled in their strength, maturity, and poise. They had grown up, and what could bring me greater joy?

In the same way, it is very sad when in the spiritual life a person remains perpetually an infant. Hebrews 5 counsels that this should not be. Apparently, the believers in verse 12 had been Christians long enough by that point to have a different level of spiritual maturity, wisdom, and discernment. In Hebrews 6:12 this same author goes on to suggest that this does not mean that God discounts or ignores what has happened in their spiritual lives; it is merely that they are not all they could have been. And the words used there have a bit of a sting to them; they suggest that if we have not matured in faith but have remained infants, it is because we have been sluggish rather than eager imitators of those who have matured in their faith.

The reasons Christians do not mature in their faith vary greatly. Some are "sluggish" (Hebrews 6:12). There are no two ways about it: they are lazy; spiritual growth and maturity seem like nothing but work to them. A. W. Tozer is right when he makes the observation, "Complacency is a deadly foe of all spiritual growth. Acute desire must be present or there will be no manifestation of Christ to His people. He waits to be wanted."[1]

I suspect that many do not have clearly before them the benefits of spiritual growth and development. The spiritual life has so often been presented to them as something that is not worth the bother; it is not something worth seeking. They do not have what Tozer describes as "acute desire" because they have not been shown something *worth* desiring. If they lack the desire for spiritual growth, it is often because they have not been helped to see that spiritual maturity is not a burden, but freedom, strength, and joy.

In the chapters that follow I hope to respond to this quandary with both encouragement and counsel. We need a fresh call to grow in faith, hope, and love, and we need practical advice on how this can happen. We need a theological grasp of the Christian life that enables us to understand more fully what it means to be "on the way." But we also need guidelines for the practice of the Christian life that will enable us to respond intentionally to the call to "grow up" in our salvation. In all of this, there are at least four things we need to keep clearly in mind.

First, we can assume that God is both calling us and enabling us to grow; we are each being invited—even summoned!—to mature in our faith, and we are at the same time given the grace and enabling for this very growth. We can assume that God is calling each of us to a deepened faith, a greater spiritual understanding, a higher integrity in our behavior, and overall greater spiritual maturity, wisdom, and discernment. And God insists on this, because only then will we really know strength, freedom, and joy. Spiritual maturity, wisdom, and discernment are not a burden; they are *freedom*. People who mature in their faith are people of strength and joy. God longs for this and aches when we are lax, sluggish, or apathetic about our spiritual condition. But God does not burden us with this; rather we are invited to respond to the call of the One who said, "My yoke is easy, and my burden is light" (Matthew 11:30). This does *not* mean that the call of God is not demanding or a challenge to us. It most certainly is that. But we must distinguish between the call and challenge to mature Christian faith and a burden. Christian maturity is not burdensome; it is freedom and strength and joy. It is health.

Second, while this call is issued to all of us, it is also appropriate to assume that we are each on a different road. We are not all called to this journey in the same way. Part of the wonder of God's grace is that the Creator speaks to each of us, calling us *individually* into greater spiritual strength and freedom. In other words, while we are called to encourage one another, be patient with one another, and bear the burden of the other, we are not called to compare ourselves to each other. Nothing is gained by either judging our neighbor or by concluding that "there is no pressure on me to grow given that others around me seem to be lax about their growth"! Rather, we are each called on our own terms—in light of our own circumstances—to respond to the invitation and enabling of God. We are each called to take responsibility for our own lives and our own rate and level of spiritual maturity.

Yes, we are part of communities. And there is no way that we can be all that we are called to be unless we are connected with others. But nothing in Scripture softens the call to personal responsibility. What we need, actually, are men and women to take active responsibility for their own lives as members of those very communities. Community does not soften or ease the call to personal responsibility. To the contrary: our life in community enables us to take a sober look at ourselves and to act conscientiously and courageously.

Third, when we speak of spiritual growth we naturally then call one another to discern the particular call and enabling of the Spirit. We encourage one another by fostering within each one the capacity to be attentive to God. We can and must each ask this of ourselves: Where and in what ways is God drawing me, prompting my heart, calling me, and enabling me to mature in my faith? Some of this spiritual growth will come without our fully being conscious of the ways in which God is at work in our lives. As we attend to the fundamental practices of the spiritual life—individually and as members of the Christian community—God grants us a measure of His grace that enables us to grow in faith, hope, and love.

And at other times, we are quite conscious of God's work, especially in times of difficulty or temptation when the growth edge of our lives is squarely before us—such as when my son was sick—and we know that nothing matters more right now than that we learn to trust God in the midst of the uncertainty and pain. At the stress points of life we can ask God the questions, What does this mean for me? How is the difficulty I am experiencing at the office an occasion for God's grace in my life? How is the challenge of raising a teenager a means of grace in my life, an opportunity not only for my child to grow, but also for me to grow? In difficulty—but also when things seem to be going well—we can always ask, How is this circumstance, at this time and place, an occasion for God's work and enabling in my life?

When one is raising a teen, the temptation is always there to pray *only* for one's son or daughter, but we also need to pray, Lord, as I pray for my teenager, may I also know the grace of having parented a teen. In other words, we are always attentive to what God is doing in *our* lives, not merely asking Him to be at work in the life of another. When I have a particularly difficult coworker at the office, it is tempting to bemoan what strikes me to be the immaturity of the other person rather than to ask God how *I* am to grow in His grace in this relationship.

Each day is packed full of possibilities. Each problem we face and difficulty we encounter is an opportunity to ask, Where is God in this? And what is God saying to me in the midst of it? And by this I do not for a moment mean to suggest that we only ask these questions in the midst of problems and difficulties or in the heat of a difficult relationship. When we experience a kind act, when a shopkeeper is particularly gracious and attentive, when we pass a police officer who is bringing care and order to a neighborhood, or when we happen upon an older person whose countenance is filled with joy, each is but another call to hear God and live in His grace.

And then, fourth, there is something else that needs to be emphasized in all of this: God does His work in His time in our lives. We do not mature ourselves; rather, we respond to the initiative and grace of God. This means that there are times of intense growth and development, but that there will also be times of quiet and seeming inactivity in our spiritual lives. But perhaps these are times when the character of God's work is different, comparable to the work of the Creator in a tree during the dark of winter. God is still creator and sustainer of His creation, but the work in winter is different from the vitality of spring. In the same way, we need to be patient with God. While attentive to His grace, we can accept that there are times in our lives when God's work is happening, but in *His* time. Sometimes we are called to be patient with God, to trust His work, and to trust His timing. We grow in freedom, strength, joy, and wisdom at a rate and in a manner congruent with God's agenda for our lives.

As we grow older, with God's grace we find that we do not resent the passing of the years but enjoy them. There are few things so wonderful in this life as meeting women and men who in their senior years have "walked with God" and have learned that what really matters in the end is not the number of accomplishments or how famous we are or how wealthy but rather the quality — not the quantity — of our accomplishments, the character of our relationships, whether we are really wise women and men, the depth of our joy — if indeed we have learned to love God and our neighbor as ourselves.

In the end, though, there is nothing that can take the place of a deep and profound *desire* to mature in our faith, on the one hand, and a resolve to do something about it, on the other. In *The Pursuit of God*, A. W. Tozer gives his readers a list of the great saints in the history of the church and then asks what it was that made them unique. In response he writes,

> I venture to suggest that the one vital quality which they had in common was spiritual receptivity. Something in them was open to heaven, something which urged them Godward. Without attempting anything like a profound analysis I shall say simply that they had spiritual awareness and that they went on to cultivate it until it became the biggest thing in their lives. They differed from the average person in that they when they felt the inward longing they did something about it. They acquired the lifelong habit of spiritual response.[2]

In other words, they had two qualities we should cultivate: receptivity and intentionality.

THE SUFFICIENCY OF GRACE

When we think about and seek to live the Christian life, we can always make a basic assumption: the sufficiency of God's grace — the reality that God is on our side and that He will enable us to be all that we are called to be. God calls us, and this calling is matched by the enabling of God. God calls us; God grants us the grace to respond to that call. And what He provides us is enough; it is that we need to be all that we are called to be. In Christ "all the fullness of the Deity lives in bodily form" (Colossians 2:9, NIV). Consequently, all we need is found in Him, and the Scriptures affirm the sufficiency of Christ for the believer in any situation. The key, though, is found in appropriating this grace for the particularities of our life situation.

In the Middle Ages, spirituality was often compared to a bridge. The bridge was meant to portray the grace of God enabling a person who, while on the way would traverse the

Christian life by moving from darkness to light, from sin to righteousness, from immaturity to maturity in their faith.
Contemporary author Joseph de Guibert suggests we can take
the image of the bridge one step further. One bridge does not fill
all situations. There are many, many varieties of bridges, with different styles and structures as well as different materials used to
build them.[3] Generally, topography, geological setting, and
specifics about the terrain will determine the kind of bridge that
engineers will design and build. But the style and form of the
bridge also reflects the resources available to the builders. There
are stone, wood, concrete, and steel bridges; there are simple
straight bridges as well as grand suspension bridges over major
canyons or rivers. The principle is simple: different terrain and
different resources require and allow for different kinds of
bridges.

In the same way, we can and should seek a form of spirituality
that is congruent with the topography of our lives. However,
materials cannot be combined at random and must be appropriate. A wooden bridge cannot cross the Golden Gate in San
Francisco. Reinforced concrete cannot be mixed with wood.
There must be consistency or, as de Guibert puts it, we need "an
organic, balanced combination of materials and shapes."[4]

The bridge image has further application. We cannot transfer
a particular bridge from one place to another. If we move to
another place, we need a new bridge for a new context that
appropriates the resources at hand. We need to adapt to different
terrain. Similarly, a spirituality needs to reflect two fundamental
factors: the context in which we live and the resources available
to us. As we move from one place to another or as there are transitions in our lives, we need to give careful consideration to the
new terrain and examine our resources—the means of grace—
that are available to us. We need to reflect upon the kind of
bridge that would be suitable for our new situation.

We can learn from the experience of previous builders and
even from our own experience, but the bridge in this new life sit-

uation will need to be designed for ourselves and for our particular challenges and opportunities in that context. We will incorporate the essential elements of a spirituality—the fundamental disciplines and practices—in a manner that is unique to our personal life situation. Obviously, some of these components will overlap with those of others living in similar "terrain"; but in the end we will have pieced together a personalized and integrated set of disciplines and practices designed so that we—as individuals in this time and in this place—can appropriate as thoroughly as possible the grace of God that enables us to be all that we are called to be. This means that we need to take ourselves seriously and ask honest questions about ourselves and our circumstances before we can design an authentic spirituality.

ACKNOWLEDGING OUR DIFFERENCES

In designing a viable spirituality, the first principle is that our spirituality needs to fit uniquely our context and resources and to reflect an organic consistency. Building on the metaphor of the bridge, we need to get the lay of the land. As well as we can, we should consider the terrain of our lives, what is unique to our circumstances and perhaps similar to others' in terms of a whole variety of criteria. Here are six of the factors that need to be considered: age or personal maturity; personality type or temperament; gender; vocation and occupation; living situation; and culture and social perspective.

First, we should definitely take account of age or personal maturity. When the apostle Paul urges Timothy to "shun youthful passions," (2 Timothy 2:22)—or as it is put in an older translation, "flee . . . youthful lusts" (KJV)—he acknowledges by implication that the struggles and temptations of a young person are different from those of a person in midlife or in the senior years. Thus the contours of a spiritual life for a person in midlife and older may well be and perhaps should be quite different, even though the basic elements will remain the same. This requires honesty, the honesty of growing older graciously, of facing up to both the limitations and the opportunities and greater responsibilities that come with growing older.

The second factor that affects a Christian spirituality is personality type or temperament. We are not the same physically; neither are we the same psychologically and emotionally. When we are made whole in Christ, the entire body of Christ manifests a wonderful diversity of personalities and temperaments, which is another way of saying that we think, react, and respond differently. And there is no reason why our spiritualities would not reflect this diversity.

Some may resist this idea that we are not the same psychologically. Many of us have grown up in spiritual communities that assumed there was a kind of *Christian* temperament, a personality or personal style that was legitimized by religious leaders and held up as the ideal. The sad part of this is that people are then so easily caught up living by pretense, with masks that they hope reflect this ideal. And they never find themselves, accept themselves, or live with a spirituality that is congruent with the contours of *their* personalities and temperaments. Part of growing in grace is accepting who God made us to be.

A third factor that for some may be equally important is gender. While it may be that we often overstate our differences as women and men, it is nevertheless true that we are not the same. While many of these differences may well be culturally conditioned, it is still appropriate to affirm that gender is a significant factor in shaping who we are and how we respond to God, one another, and our world. Having said this, it is also appropriate to affirm that we should learn from one another. We can seek a spirituality that is congruent with whether we are men or women, but we cannot press this too far. In many respects I am growing in my appreciation for the fact that women have a lot to teach me about what it means to be a follower of Jesus Christ.

Fourth, it is also appropriate that we appreciate that vocation and occupation shape our spiritualities. The spirituality of a medical doctor will probably appear to be quite different from that of a mother at home caring for small children. Much spiritual literature over the centuries has been written by those who have given themselves to a life of prayer and contemplation. Today we can celebrate recent publications that have enabled us to more fully consider what it means to foster a spirituality that enables us to be in the marketplace, for example. In all of this what we can appreciate is that the character of our work in the world can and indeed must shape the contours of our spirituality.

What we seek is a spirituality appropriate for our vocations. The principles of the spiritual life are the same, but the way they are practiced will vary. And thus we must ask, What is a spirituality appropriate to the challenges and temptations of my vocation and work? If I am an artist, for example, what are the unique stress points to which I need to be conscious as I seek the grace of God for my life and work? If I am in business—struggling to sustain a small operation or, conversely, wildly successful and now more conscious than ever of how much money I am making—what does this mean for the contours of my spirituality? What, we can each ask, is the spirituality that will enable me to exploit the opportunities I have (rather than complain about what I do not have) and enable me to know grace in response to the particular temptations and difficulties I face because of the character of my work.

Fifth, one's living situation may well be one of the most crucial factors shaping a spirituality. My own search to identify the essential elements of a Christian spirituality came with my move from a small Canadian city to the large metropolis of Manila. This move included a change of roles and responsibilities from a pastoral ministry to theological education. Further, it was also a time in which my wife and I now had two small children. Each of these was necessarily a factor to which I needed to adapt and to which I needed to respond.

When we make a geographic move or when a change in our life circumstances is forced upon us, we are wise only when we honestly ask what it means to have a spirituality that is congruent with a new situation. It seems particularly naïve, for example, for someone to move from rural Iowa to New York City and not realize that inherent in this move is a demand that he or she consider what it means to have a spirituality that takes full account of the call to live in the city, in an urban context. Of course, part of the challenge of this is that so much Christian spirituality seems to assume pastoral or rural images of that spiritual life. But most of us live in cities, and many of us have moved there and only later begun to appreciate that the spiritual life will look and feel different in such an environment.

Finally, culture and social perspective will be a factor in any spirituality. Failure to recognize this is often the cause of much misunderstanding and frequently blocks a Christian community from developing a truly indigenous spiritual life. Of course we also have much to learn from one another across cultures. We are part of a global community now, and this presents us with wonderful opportunities to learn from other cultures and societies in ways inconceivable to Christians of previous generations. We have the opportunity to read the devotional works of writers who come from other countries and cultures, but we also must take advantage of those times when we are able to be in conversation with those whose background, culture, and ethnicity is different from our own. We will as often as not find that they will challenge our assumptions; in surprising ways they will rekindle our imaginations and restore our hope. They will call us to see Jesus through a different set of lenses. So while we need a spirituality that is congruent with our cultural circumstances, this is never meant to imply that we are not always in a posture of learning from those whose culture and ethnicity are different from our own.

All of these individual considerations should free us from feeling obligated or burdened by the spiritual pattern of our neighbor. One person's conscience and vision of the spiritual life may lead him or her up one path or across one bridge—and we do not all need to follow. On the other hand, this principle reminds us that each of us is responsible for his or her own spiritual walk. No one else can design this for us; there is no simple how-to manual. Though there are friends and pastors and colleagues along the way, this is a matter we ultimately need to resolve for ourselves.

ACCEPTING CHANGE GRACIOUSLY

All of this means that we can develop an authentic spirituality only if we pay attention to the changes in our lives, both exterior and interior. But more, it also means that we need to graciously accept the change that comes our way. Change is as much a part of human life as current is to a river. For some, this makes life a problem and a burden; they just wish that things would stay the same. They value the continuities of life and find their solace in those things that remain as they have been. And they fear change. But we cannot stop change; and nothing is gained by resisting the challenges time brings us.

We face changes in our families as our children grow older. With the passing of years, we inevitably come to terms with changes in the workplace, in our work and ministry, in our churches, and in the pattern of our relationships. Some changes should be resisted, of course; but I am speaking here of the changes that are part of the very fabric of life. We are wise only when we accept these changes graciously and then adjust and adapt our spirituality to these new developments—whatever they might be. I find it helpful to think in terms of "chapters" of our lives as a way not only to accept change but also to affirm that there is a change. My sons grow up and move out of the house. I leave one position and accept another, and then realize that everything I learned about the spiritual life in my last job may have applied to that set of circumstances, but now I have a whole different set of circumstances that requires a willingness on my part to adapt and adjust.

Naturally, the ideal is that we accept a change as a new opportunity and challenge, that we see how change gives God an opportunity to develop another side of our character such that with each new development the Spirit is given opportunity to call us into another dimension of what it means to be a disciple of Jesus Christ. I find the story of the prophet Elijah particularly interesting in this respect, partly because it highlights not only his extraordinary faith, but also because we see in him an honest wrestling with the changes in his life circumstances. He demonstrates for us that faith may look very different as we move on to the next chapter of our lives. In 1 Kings 17–18, Elijah has the faith to see and believe that God would feed a widow and bring her son back to life and later that He would visibly demonstrate His truth through the confrontation with the false prophets at Mount Carmel. But then in chapter 19 we have a very different Elijah, one who hears God speak not in the visible demonstration of power he saw at the top of Carmel, but rather in the "sound of sheer silence" (1 Kings 19:12). What God calls him to is the ordinary and mundane duties of a prophet. His experience is a reminder for me that we all need faith and that the expression of faith will have a different character for different chapters of our lives. God will certainly call us to trust Him in times of momentous decisions and transitions, as Elijah was called to trust God at Mount Carmel. At other times, we are called to trust God in the ordinary and the mundane as we complete and perform our daily duties and responsibilities with patience and grace.

Paying Attention

We are wise, then, to welcome and consider the biblical admonition, as Paul puts it to Timothy: "Pay close attention to yourself" (1 Timothy 4:16). The human mind and heart are exceedingly complex. As the Spirit of God performs divine surgery on our inner persons, transforming us into the image of God, He does so within (and through) our geographic and social contexts. Changes in our life circumstances tend to unearth and reveal dimensions of our lives of which we were probably unaware.

By saying we need to pay attention to ourselves, I am not for a moment suggesting that we are not paying attention to God. To the contrary: the wonder of the spiritual life at this point is that we *cannot* pay attention to God *unless* we learn to pay attention to ourselves. Our own lives and the circumstances of our lives are the very lens by which we attend to the work of God, particularly God's gracious initiative in our lives. God's work in our lives never occurs in a vacuum; it always finds expression within the actual particularities of living situations, the challenges of work, the vicissitudes of life, the vulnerabilities and anxieties we feel—through both health and sickness, problems and opportunities.

Even if we do not experience external transitions and developments in our lives, it is still essential that we pay attention to our thoughts, motives, and behavior. It is helpful to acknowledge—through regular self-examination—the areas in our lives that God would like to transform and then to seek to respond adequately and creatively, and yes, even eagerly.

Ideally, the different elements of the spiritual life should fit together into an organic whole in the life of the individual Christian. This book provides the ingredients, but the reader must decide how much of each ingredient needs to be included in his or her spirituality. A new Christian may feel the need to stress the renewal of the mind; another may see the present chapter of her life as one in which she appreciates her need for extensive times of personal encounter with God; a third person may recognize that at this point in his life, he requires formal, spiritual direction. The point is this: we need to design a spirituality for ourselves that adequately allows us to appropriate God's grace for spiritual growth and vitality in our *present* living and working situation. We want to be alive in the here and now.

Again, the elements of the spiritual life might be compared to the components that make up the construction of a bridge. In different contexts or settings, the elements will be put in place and combined with others in a manner that fits that person at that time and in that place.

God's grace is sufficient (2 Corinthians 12:9). This is a truth we need to reaffirm again and again. We have a tremendous promise within God's Word—that His grace is sufficient for whatever our situation. God will never give us a ravine that is too wide or deep for us to build a bridge across; further, He will always provide us with the needed resources.

We may get frustrated trying to find good books to read or despair that we will not hear the Word of God preached effectively. We may feel very alone and think that a spiritual director is something we cannot possibly find. But we need to temper these feelings with an abiding conviction that though we may lack what we think we need, God has promised to be our provision. In response to this promise, we need to open our eyes with gratitude and make every effort to respond to what He does provide.

And we must appropriate His grace; we must live in conscious awareness of the means of grace that God has provided. Good books to read—we may need to pay a price. A faithful preacher of the Word—we may need to listen more carefully and willingly to the preacher God has provided. A good spiritual director—we may need to travel and be near him or her for several days. Again, there may be a price to pay. But we cannot presume upon God's grace. God will sustain us as we appropriate the means of grace He provides.

THE RENEWAL OF THE MIND

Spiritual writers will have varied emphases as they describe the spiritual life, and they will differ on what matters most or is most crucial in the formation of a Christian spirituality. Some will emphasize the place of prayer as the pivot on which the whole of the Christian life rests. For others, the heart of the matter will be one's identification with a cause or a people, whether it be a commitment to evangelism and mission for some or identification with the poor, such as those who write about the spiritual life out of the perspective of liberation theology. And yet others will speak of our identification with the church and our capacity to be loved and love others within Christian community. However, though we may debate what is most important in the *end*, there is no argument on where we need to *begin:* with the renewal of the mind. Nothing is more crucial than that we learn to *think* Christianly. Everything else in the Christian life depends on our capacity to allow truth to engage our minds from top to bottom, inside and out. And so, though it might be argued that this is not the most important element of the Christian life, here is where we must start.

LEARNING TO THINK CHRISTIANLY

If we are going to be in but not of the world—as women and men who live in union with Christ and who grow in our capacity to live in joy even in a broken world, maturing in faith, hope, and love—then it is imperative that we learn to think Christianly. Everything depends on this. To walk in the Spirit requires a spiritual mind. Our transformation into the image of God is dependent on renewed minds (Romans 12:2). The Bible calls us to love God with our whole minds. Consequently, *the* critical component of a Christian spirituality is care for one's thinking, paying attention to the diverse ways in which God is enabling us to be made new by the truth.

The Bible calls for the renewal of the mind. We find this throughout Scripture, but the call is most notable in the writings of Paul. It is in his letters that we find the exhortation to "be transformed by the renewing of your minds" (Romans 12:2). The apostle also urges us not to be taken captive through deceptive philosophy, which he identifies as the basic principles of this world (Colossians 2:8). We cannot grow in Christ if we allow the world to shape the way we think, if our values, mores, and worldviews are determined by our culture.

The Bible therefore calls us to turn. Repentance includes turning in the way we think—a change of mind. Those who are not in Christ are described by Paul as darkened in the way they think; those who are in Christ are urged to set their minds on things above (Colossians 3:2), being renewed in knowledge after the image of the Creator (3:10). This involves allowing the Word of Christ to dwell richly within the mind (3:16). This is conversion—the turning from an unspiritual mind (2:18), with the goal that every thought be taken captive and made obedient to Christ (2 Corinthians 10:5).

What we think is what we are and what we will become. Unless we are renewed in the attitudes of our mind—in the way we think—we cannot hope to become what God would have us to be. The mind is the steering wheel of the person. It is only as our minds are renewed and controlled by the Spirit of God that we can hope to become mature in our faith.

Some may think that the call for a renewed mind only applies to intellectuals or academics, that it does not apply to the common person. But Paul makes no such distinction between the intelligent and the not-so-intelligent. Rather, Scripture assumes that all people have intelligence. That is what it means to be a person—a thinking, rational being. (By this I am not for a moment suggesting that those who are mentally ill or mentally handicapped are not full persons. Not for a moment. It is rather that we recognize and long for the new heavens and the new earth, when God will make all things well and grant to them something that is so fundamental to their humanity—the capacity to think deeply, critically, and creatively.)

The Bible assumes that the human mind is a wondrous thing. St. Augustine captures this well when he speaks of the memory and the imagination.

> Men go forth to marvel at the mountain heights, at huge waves in the sea, at the broad expanse of flowing rivers, at the wide reaches of the ocean, and at the circuit of the stars, but themselves they pass by. They do not marvel at the fact that while I was speaking of these things I did not look upon them with my own eyes.[1]

They fail to appreciate that their own minds and their own capacities to see and imagine and picture these realities are such incredible things. God has given us an extraordinary gift—the capacity to think, imagine, consider, understand, and know. Most of all, every Christian can come to love God with the whole mind. Each person can come to have a mind renewed according to the image of Christ. The renewal of the mind is a concern much broader than the intellectual or academic life in a culture. Academic study is unquestionably helpful. But when we speak of the renewal of the mind, we affirm the critical need for all people to think Christianly, biblically, and deeply. And we affirm that it is possible. Everyone has a good mind. And for everyone the principle remains the same: it is only as our minds are transformed that we are able to discern the will of God and to know what is "good and acceptable and perfect" (Romans 12:2).

If we are going to live in this world without being caught up in its patterns of thought and behavior, our minds need to be renewed. If we are going to live in union with Christ, we are going to have to think in radically different categories. And if we are going to live in emotional maturity as women and men of joy even in a broken world, it all begins with allowing truth to percolate into the inner recesses of our hearts and minds. It begins with learning how to think Christianly.

Few people give conscious thought to what is happening in their minds. Thinking is not usually something we think about! We just do it. And that is part of the problem; we take it for granted or assume that attention to the mind does not in itself require discipline. However, we will not be renewed in the way we think unless we give it serious attention. It requires some intentionality and discipline. It will mean, at the very least, that we are attentive to two things: first, the renewal of the *way* in which we think, and second, *what* we think about, the focus of our thoughts. The full and extended renewal of the mind involves both dimensions.

At the center of this intentionality comes a resolve that we will seek the truth, love the truth, and live by the truth. A commitment to our minds presupposes this resolve. It presumes that we care about truth, that truth is not something we fear but long for. And we seek the truth because we know that health, strength, and freedom come through the truth. We know that ignorance is no bliss, but hell!

To pursue the truth is to seek to see things as God sees them. To live truthfully requires that we begin to see the world, ourselves, our society, our past, and our future as God sees these realities. And this will not happen unless we are alert and intentionally attentive to what is happening in our minds. On the one hand, this demands that we accept with humility where our thinking is misguided and wrong; it requires the grace to accept that our thinking may well be completely misguided, that before we came to Christ our thinking was warped, and that even as Christians we cannot assume that we see the world as God sees the world.

In coming to Christ, we urgently need a complete and comprehensive turnaround in our thinking. Beforehand we saw and thought and understood things, but we did not see reality in the right perspective. Our thinking lacked the most important dimension—God. Growth in grace, therefore, means growing up and turning around in the way we think. It means coming to a deeper and fuller understanding of the truth, the way God sees things. We can only live in freedom when we see and understand as God does. In other words, we need to adopt a Christian worldview. But this does not happen in a moment; rather, in coming to Christ we turn and begin the slow process of incrementally allowing the truth to inform and reform our thinking.

We need to be renewed in the way we think, but also in the *focus* of our thoughts—what we think about. We are called by Paul to "think about these things": the true, the noble, the right, the pure, the lovely, the admirable, the excellent . . . all that is "worthy of praise" (Philippians 4:8). If we are what we think, it follows that we are wise to be intentional about the focus and character of our thoughts.

The mind is an amazing thing. It is our most private space. When it comes to the focus of our thoughts, we are all individuals standing alone and choosing what we will think about. A doctor can look inside my body and tell me what my heart is doing and what my kidneys are doing. But the mind is my private space. The mind is also amazing in that it never stops working. It is active even when we sleep. The mind is affecting the direction of our lives even when we are not thinking about such profound questions.

But what do we think about? What passes through our thoughts when we are riding the bus to our place of work or going to a store to do some shopping? What is happening in our minds when we are just waiting? It is at these times as much as any other that we need to recognize the importance of discipline. We cannot know the peace of God and be renewed in our thinking unless we allow the Spirit of God to control our minds. And this includes consciously directing our thoughts to that which is "worthy of praise" (Philippians 4:8).

Even as we sleep at night, the mind will focus on those thoughts that dominate our thinking before we actually fall asleep. We are therefore urged to give special attention to these moments in the day and to settle our thoughts—possibly through the Word—on that which is good, honorable, and just.

Our goal is the biblical ideal of a renewed mind, what Scripture identifies as the mind of Christ. Such a mind is sustained and enabled by truth. Armando Valladares was imprisoned for twenty-three years in the brutal, inhuman Cuban prison system. He languished there year after year, suffering incredible abuse because of his convictions. He refused to compromise with his accusers and consequently faced the fury of a regime intolerant of dissenters. How did he survive with sound mind and spirit for twenty-three years? His biography, *Against All Hope*, provides at least part of the answer.[2] On the one hand, we are struck by his faith in God as the anchor of his thoughts and reactions. This in turn found expression in his personal commitment to live by his conscience, to persist in hope, and finally in his willingness to forgive his tormentors. On the other hand, in reading his story what impresses the reader was his attentiveness to his thinking, to his mind, to what happened in his mind. He knew that his only hope of survival was that he would by God's grace keep his mind focused on the truth, even when everything around him was threatening all he found precious. He demonstrates for me that even in remarkable suffering and difficulty, we can still assume responsibility for our own minds—for how we think and for the focus of our thoughts. It is really up to us, but it requires discipline, attentiveness, and intentionality.

And to the degree that we learn to think Christianly, we will find that the mind is pervaded by peace, a peace that "surpasses all understanding" (Philippians 4:7). But this characteristic feature of the Christian mind only comes to those who choose to live in joy — not in anxiety — casting their cares upon God. The peace of God is a gift to those who discipline their minds to think on those things that are worthy of praise.

TEMPTATION, THE MIND, AND THE SPIRIT

Comment also needs to be made about temptation, a common experience. We all are tempted: no one is exempt. Though temptation will take on different forms for different people and though in frank discussion we may find that where one experiences temptation, the other seemingly feels no inclination, all of us are tempted. Temptation could simply be understood as the inclination to *not* live by our conscience, by what we know is right, true, and good. Or, another way to see it is as the inclination to conclude that sin is not so bad after all, that sin is not a matter of life and death. Temptation is the inclination *not* to take sin seriously.

However, we do not live in truth unless we appreciate that sin is a matter of life and death. In Genesis 2:17 we have the explicit statement of God that if the first parents of humanity ate of the forbidden fruit, they would die. The snake came visiting and suggested to the contrary, that if they ate of the fruit they would not die. So they believed the snake, ate the fruit, and the consequence was death of such a pervasive and horrific depth that the whole created order was alienated from the life of God.

Since then the Evil One has been doing the same work. Every temptation is a suggestion that sin is not really so bad, not really so terrible as the Bible states, not really a matter of life and death. But God's law is a law of life; the righteousness of God is the substance of life — freedom in peace and joy. Therefore, anything that violates the law of God is death — however attractive it may seem at first glance, however much we may seemingly long for it, crave it, and feel we cannot live without it — it is death. Sin is death, any way you look at it. Romans 8:13 is, then, a sobering reality, but also good news: "For if you live according to the flesh, you will die; but if by the Spirit you put to death the deeds of the body, you will live."

Holiness, then, is a matter of life and death. So what will it take for us to know and live the truth, to stand firm in response to temptation? I am convinced it will take three things: an assurance that we are loved; radical dependence on the Spirit; and an understanding that it all begins in the mind. First, we need to have a deep and abiding assurance that we are loved. We need to know that we are no longer under condemnation (Romans 8:1). If we fear condemnation, we will not be able to grow in the grace of God. But more, we also need to know that we are accepted as the children of God. The inner witness of the Spirit grants us the essential assurance that God has called us into His company (Romans 8:14-17). This precondition is not secondary or incidental. We will never grow in personal and corporate holiness if we doubt the love and acceptance of God. It only comes if we know that we are forgiven, accepted, and loved by God.

Second, our capacity to respond to temptation calls for radical dependence on the Spirit. God's passion for holiness is powerfully evident in the wonderful gift of the Spirit, the Spirit of holiness, the Spirit of life. Without this gift, there is no hope. In our weakened human condition—fallen in sin—we are incapable of holiness, incapable of fulfilling the purposes and expectations of God, incapable of living. Our only hope is through the indwelling Spirit. Indeed, there are few things so central to a biblical notion of holiness as the affirmation that we do not sanctify ourselves. It is the work of the Spirit. But it is a slow, incremental process by which the Spirit enables us to respond well to temptation and grow in grace. It may be a slow, uphill struggle against sin. We are weak. But in Christ the battle has begun and in Christ nothing will allow us to turn back from our resolve to be free of the oppression of sin and free in God's holiness. God gives us a passion for life.

Third, we have no obligation to this fallen state, as the apostle puts it: "But if Christ is in you, though the body is dead because of sin, the Spirit is life because of righteousness" (Romans 8:10). We have no logical necessity or need to live according to this fallen condition. We can, by the Spirit, turn the corner. We can be men and women who are a living testimony to a God who indwells people and who by His grace enables them to overcome the power of sin and death. We can, but it is not automatic. If we live out of an awareness of the love of God and in radical dependence upon the Spirit, it all comes back to what is happening in the *mind*. We are faced with a radical choice that is laid out for us by Paul in Romans 8:5: "For those who live according to the flesh set their minds on the things of the flesh, but those who live according to the Spirit set their minds on the things of the Spirit." Then, as verse 6 reminds us, the mind of sin is death whereas the mind controlled by the Spirit is life and peace.

Here is the crux of the matter: it all begins in the *mind*. We can hardly overstate this. The human person is so designed that it cannot have two fundamental orientations at the same time. We need to choose between them. What the apostle portrays for us here are two entirely different ways of viewing life. The one sees the whole of life in terms of the material, the worldly—what he calls the flesh, or the "mind of sinful man" (NIV). The other sees the whole of life in terms of the spiritual, the eternal. The one is the mind of death; the other, the mind of life. The first thinks in a way that cannot please God; the other's thinking is in tune with the Spirit.

The mind of the flesh is independent, self-centered, and opposed to the will of God. The mind of the Spirit mirrors the mind of Christ, who gave Himself for others. Yes, we are still fallen humanity. We are still in the flesh. But though we are in this condition, that reality is not the primary factor that shapes who we are, who we serve, and how we live. By the enabling of the Spirit, our outlook, our perspective on life has changed so that we are focused toward God and the things of God. We are in the flesh but we do not live according to the flesh. We live in the Spirit.

The choice is ours. Will we, in our *thinking*, actively respond to the initiatives of our fallen natures or will we respond to the inner prompting of the Spirit? There is no life in the Spirit apart from a conscious, deliberate, and intentional effort to walk in the Spirit, to *think* in response to the prompting of the Spirit, and to act in obedience to the law of God.

All sin begins in the mind; all holiness begins there also. With every temptation, every subtle or explicit inclination to violate the will of God, the crucial question is what we will *think*. We are not able to be holy except by the enabling of the Spirit. But the Spirit cannot enable and bear His fruit in us if we do not turn from sin in our minds.

When temptation is overpowering, it is simply because we have allowed the temptation to settle in our minds. We have longed for this, or craved that, or fantasized in our minds about the other until we are incapable of handling the temptation. We lose or win the battle in the mind.

If you start to complain, make a mindful decision to turn from the posture of complaint; dispel the complaining with gratitude. If in your mind you are longing for more and more, and you sense that greed, a pattern of comparison with others, or discontent is dominating your thoughts, then turn and choose the way of contentment, with gratitude. If your mind takes you away from faithfulness to your spouse, turn in your thinking to that which is good, noble, and worthy of praise. When jealousy or envy arise, it is so important that you turn and pray for the other person and ask that God would bless him or her. When fear arises in your heart, turn from worry to trust. Temptation will come, and in freedom we need to turn, turn in our thoughts, and reject what is not of God.

The only conceivable way in which we can respond to temptation is by a choice to set our minds on the things of the Spirit, convinced that in the Spirit we find life, whereas in the flesh we live in death. This is, of course, an act of faith. We think on these things, but the work of transforming us is that of the Spirit. Holiness is the Spirit's fruit.

Therefore, we need to remember something. By faith we allow the Spirit to mold us and direct us and transform us according to His schedule. We are in the flesh, and we will therefore continue to fail. Though we love the Lord with all our hearts, we will continually be amazed at how stupid we can be, how foolish, and how sinful. But as we trust God and set our minds on the things of the Spirit, He will—in His good and perfect timing—bear His fruit in us.

Many talk like the Spirit's work is instantaneous, and often I wonder if the call for revival that we often hear is much like a call for instant results. But more often than not, the work of the Spirit is quiet, incremental, and steady. The work of God will never happen as quickly as we would like. But our faith allows us and enables us to affirm that God is working, the Spirit is indwelling, and by the grace of God we are, each day, different people, not by our efforts or ingenuity, but because of the Spirit's work in our lives. So we set our minds on the things of the Spirit. And God's passion for life will be our passion as well.

THE BUILDING BLOCKS FOR A CHRISTIAN MIND

To think Christianly is to see and respond to everything in terms of Christ: His incarnation, crucifixion, and exaltation. That is, we think *historically*. We think and live in terms of our contemporary historical context, but specifically and intentionally in terms of the history of the person and work of Jesus Christ—past, present, and future: His life, death, and resurrection in the past; His presence among us now by His Spirit; and His triumph and reign both now and in the future with His personal return and consummation of His kingdom. It must be Jesus who defines what it means to *think* Christianly and thus what it means to be a

Christian. This means that we take the Incarnation and the Cross seriously.

The Incarnation and the Christian Mind

The Incarnation is the declaration by God of the unique identity of Jesus Christ—both completely *man* and also wholly *God*. First, with the Incarnation, God meets us and knows us and invites us to Himself. With the Incarnation, true spirituality is necessarily centered in Jesus and finds meaning and purpose in terms of Jesus. He broke the impasse between heaven and earth, making a relationship with God possible.

Second, the reality of the Incarnation is also a reminder that the Christian life is a response to God in the church. The church is the body of Christ—the visible, living presence of the incarnate Lord in the world. Christ communicates His Word and grace through the ministry of the church—specifically, the corporate life and ministry of believers, the preaching and teaching of the Word, the sacraments, prayer, and worship. True spirituality is not merely oriented to the individual. It is life in community.

Third, the Incarnation makes it very plain that a true spirituality is a response to God in the world. On the one hand, this implies that the world is created by God and is intended to be the sphere of God's rule. A Christian mind is one that takes the material world seriously, recognizing that all of God's creation is a demonstration of the glory of God. But more, the Incarnation is a reminder that true spirituality finds expression in the world. Through Christ, God intends to bring all things under His kingdom rule, and this "all things" means the whole of His creation. True spirituality, then, is not escapist. We cannot view the Christian life as something lived outside of this world or in anticipation of an otherworldly kingdom. Our salvation is very earthly. A true spirituality is driven by a concern to find visible expression of God's goodness and justice in the world. A spirituality that encourages an abandonment of the world cannot be called Christian.

Fourth, an incarnational spirituality recognizes that there is a need for structure, order, and routine in the Christian life. We are not angels. We are flesh and blood creatures, and therefore our understanding of spirituality need make no apology for our physical state. This is how we were created. In affirming our bodies, we need to recognize that our very humanity must define our spirituality. When we pray, we do not pray as angels. We are embodied souls.

A spirituality that fails to recognize and appreciate our full humanity inadvertently denies that Christ Jesus came in the flesh. An affirmation of Christ's humanity—and therefore our own—frees us to appreciate the significance of space and time for the Christian life. Each of the acts by which we appropriate the grace of God is essentially an action of our bodies—our whole beings—in space and time; they are specific, tangible disciplines and practices that we do in response to God's grace. We are embodied souls and so we need structure, routine, and order to properly nurture our relationship with the living God and our kingdom activity in the world.

The Crucified Mind

To think Christianly it is imperative that we learn to think and act and respond to our world in the light of the crucifixion of our Lord Jesus Christ. But, it is not that we think in terms of this objective reality merely as light to our lives; we must go further and learn what it means to have a mind that is thoroughly identified with the Cross: a "crucified mind." This is a phrase I borrow from Kosuke Koyama, who suggests that much of Western Christianity, as it has encountered the East, has been governed by a *crusading* mind that embodies many of the ideals of Western culture with its aggressiveness and sense of manifest destiny. But as Koyama notes, this attitude of mind is utterly opposed to the gospel.[3] This is so because nothing so defines what it means to think Christianly as the reality of the Cross. Christian spirituality is the walk of faith in response to the act of Christ, which centers on His death on the cross followed by His resurrection. The Cross becomes the central point in the history of the human race. More precisely, it becomes the single most important point of reference for the person who claims to love and serve the living God. Consequently, the cross is the central symbol of our faith.

The Cross is a perpetual reminder that salvation is a gift. Christ loved us while we yet hated Him. We do not need to perform, achieve, or impress. The more we try to impress, the more our performance merely blinds us to God's love and the reality that we are accepted. Christian spirituality rests on this conviction. Spirituality is not—ever—an attempt to impress God or to earn His love. It is rather the life of faith lived in assurance of divine acceptance.

Yet more, the Cross speaks of a new order of existence. In becoming a believer, the Christian continues to be the same person. In describing what it means to become a Christian, some overstate the effects of believing in Christ and neglect the reality that we are still sinners. In other words, it is misleading to speak of this change as so thorough and effective that we no longer know the consequence of sin. Even after we have believed in Jesus, we are still fundamentally the same people. We are still sinners. However—and this is the key—this reality has been undermined! We are the same, yet we are different. In a fundamental and unsettling sense, the kingdom of light has launched a mission upon our dark hearts. We are the same people, but we have turned—we have turned to the light.

To think and live in the light of the Cross is to think as a *disciple*. The meaning of discipleship is captured in the call of Jesus, "Come, follow me." Discipleship is a response to, and a subsequent loyalty to, a *person*. Discipleship includes loyalty to a creed, to a movement, and possibly to a congregation. But ultimately, its true meaning lies in loyalty to Jesus. It is loyalty to the Jesus who was crucified and invites us to also bear the cross. In other words, discipleship is not cheap. There is a sense in which salvation is free—we cannot pay for or earn grace—yet there is another sense in which it is costly.

A few years ago a visiting evangelist to the city of Manila advertised for his mass gatherings with a slogan: "The price of admission is the same as the price of salvation—it's free." But is salvation that free? Does it actually cost us nothing? Though the gift of salvation is freely given, the New Testament message is that salvation is actually very costly. It will cost you your life. The disciples who followed Jesus left everything. In calling our fellow men and women to Christ, we must beware of misleading them. The call of Christ is to follow Him, and in following we leave our former lives behind. There is no full and authentic Christian spirituality that is not built on this principle.

This call to discipleship is a call to a new order of existence—kingdom life. It is a call to know and live in the kingdom of God. It is a call to life! Jesus came proclaiming the kingdom—characterized as the kingdom of light and salvation, a kingdom ruled by the Lord of life. This new order of existence is patterned on a new value structure, a new purpose for living, and a new basis for seeking and knowing life. For Jesus, those who seek life will lose it; those who lose it for His sake will find it. Many who are last will be first; the meek, Jesus says, will inherit the earth.

Further, to walk in the light of the Cross as a disciple of Jesus means that we think about our lives in the world in light of the mission of Jesus. In imagery that was so meaningful to the first disciples, Jesus promised that He would make them fishers of men. The gospel of Matthew concludes with a mandate: Make disciples. The mission of Christ is more than just disciple-making, but it is surely at the heart of His kingdom work—identifying with Jesus in the task of bringing men and women into a relationship of obedience, loyalty, and life—a new order of existence in the kingdom.

Someone may ask, "Is it possible to be a Christian and not be a disciple?" The answer is clear: a Christian is a disciple. That is what it means to be a Christian: to follow Christ as His disciple.

Any teaching that bypasses this principle is not true to Scripture. Any teaching that fails to uphold the call to discipleship ultimately undermines the reality of the Cross, for the One who died rose again as Lord. The One who calls us to His banquet is the King. If we come, we submit. If we love, we obey. Christian spirituality is the walk of a disciple in faith and in response to the call of Christ to lay down our lives.

The crucified One is, of course, the ascended Lord. So it follows that if our minds are informed by the life and work of Jesus Christ, we will think about this world in light of an invisible reality: Christ sits on the throne of the universe as the ascended Christ, whose complete and pervasive authority is the most important fact of the entire cosmos. To think Christianly is to see the whole of our lives in terms of this invisible reality; it means that we live and act and think and react and make choices and live our relationships in the light of Christ's kingdom rule in this world. This is the lens through which the whole of life is seen. This is what it means to live by faith.

The Mind and Television

However, does this vision of reality—the incarnate, crucified, and risen Lord—truly shape the way we think? Is Jesus Christ the fundamental reality that shapes our existence? Is faith in Christ the lens through which we view everything else?

To answer this, we must ask another question. What is it that shapes the human mind? By its very nature, the mind is conditioned by outside stimuli; it is not self-contained. The mind can only think in terms of what we feed into it. For instance, a computer is a wonderful thing. But it is useless unless it has a powerful and helpful program that can be downloaded into the system. Similarly, the mind functions constantly on the basis of what we allow it to receive. Part of personal discipline is determining what will and what will not enter our minds.

We need to decide: will our minds be filled with the values and perspectives of our society and culture (that is, the world), or will our minds be richly indwelt by the Word of God? Our minds are being shaped by outside influences whether we are conscious of it or not.

Christians in the twenty-first century need to deal with the issue of television viewing. The television is the most significant shaper of the mind in many contemporary societies. It is one of the most powerful forces in the battle for the mind, and the mind of the Christian is often a battleground between the television and its values and the impact of Scripture and its kingdom values.

Jeanne Cover is one of many critics of our day who call us to recognize that TV advertising and most TV programming essentially desensitize our vision and imagination and subtly form our priorities. The problem, Cover argues, is that the values portrayed through the television medium are nonbiblical. Commitment in marriage is trivialized, religion is downplayed, illicit relationships are accepted, violence is condoned, and a variety of commercial products are portrayed as essential for personal dignity, happiness, meaning, and success. While it is true that television may well reflect the breakdown of family life and commitment in relationships, the unnerving truth is that TV advertising and programming legitimize this deterioration. Cover concludes, "We have now come to accept the priorities and attitudes of the powerful that permeate our televised lives—success, affluence, private property, efficiency and competition, consumerism, and the 'advantages' of technology. The marketplace precepts have come to be given a universal validity."[4] In other words, the television does not merely entertain. It creates attitudes and priorities, and it portrays a view of life dominated by consumerism.

Television is essentially an entertainment medium. Many attempt to use it for other purposes. Jacques Cousteau used television to bring people to an awareness of the oceans of the world; TV evangelists seek to lead people to a knowledge of Christ. But it remains an entertainment medium. As Neil Postman so cogently notes, to use television as an educational medium is as absurd as using a 747 airplane to deliver mail between New York City and Newark (twin cities). It is the wrong medium for the purpose.[5]

Television is imagistic. Our analytical, linear thought processes are bypassed. We do not think when we watch television. We are entertained. We are passive recipients of whatever is shown to us. Therefore the influence of television, then, is not only subtle and direct, it is also pervasive, and to a remarkable degree, subconscious. It permeates the mind and radically affects the way in which a person perceives the world and discriminates between good and evil.

This has particular relevance as we wrestle with the reality of sexual drive and marital fidelity. Television blatantly and subtly caters to prurient sexual interests and curiosity. It trivializes our God-given sexuality and makes it mundane by affirming immediate gratification. Television advertising panders to our greed, our desire to impress, and our longing for comfort and amenities. Rarely does TV advertising assume we are intelligent, thinking persons. Rather, its purpose is to bypass our rational faculties and persuade us to buy or consume something, regardless of whether we really need to.

What is alarming is that this happens when our guard is down, when we are being "entertained." For many, it comes after a difficult day of work. Television is an evening activity for relaxation and leisure. It may be the single most significant influence on the way people think, even Christians. Their devotional life, their participation in public worship (including the sermon), and other valuable input such as Bible study cannot offset the far more pervasive influence of television. In other words, television is the dominant stimuli and shaper of their lives, so much so that they cannot be richly indwelt by the Word. We are no longer shocked by violence we repeatedly see; we are no longer shamed by sexual explicitness; through repeated viewing we learn to laugh at that which is explicitly contrary to our declared values. As we respond to the call to renew the minds, we must then seriously consider what it is that shapes the way we think.

A Mind Informed by Truth

Physically, we develop appetites for certain foods. A body that is fed on sweets craves sweets. Some time ago my wife, Joella, decided it was not good to have so much salt in our family's diet. So she resolved to gradually cut our salt intake over a short period of time to a bare minimum. At first I thought food would be tasteless without salt, that like all other spices, salt was essential for flavor. But I learned otherwise; I am enjoying my food as much as ever, but without the harmful effects of too much salt. Now I am amazed at how people pour salt on their food; when I eat food that has too much salt, I find it difficult to consume. Similarly, I no longer take sugar in my tea or coffee. I resolved to go off this unnecessary sweet, and now my taste buds no longer crave sugar.

The same applies to the intellect. When we feed our minds with junk food, then naturally we develop an appetite for it. It is not good to saturate our minds with television imagery, with its violence, sexual explicitness, and bland humor.

An appetite for truth—for the good, the noble, and the honorable—takes time to develop. But we cannot hope to have renewed minds unless we resolve to desire that which is good and true, unless we allow the Spirit to transform our intellectual appetites. The most important way by which the mind is renewed is through the Scriptures. Paul calls us to a mind renewed after the image of its Creator largely by letting the Word of Christ dwell richly in our minds (Colossians 3:10,16). There is more to the full renewal of the mind than only the indwelling of Scripture. The arts, travel, study within the humanities and the sciences, good conversation, and much more contribute to a renewed mind. But nothing is so basic and central as the Bible. Through the Scriptures, God has provided us with *His* perspective on life. We are free in the way we think only when we think according to the truth. The renewal of the mind is intimately linked with the knowledge of God through His Word.

This must be a pervasive and experiential knowledge. It is not merely a matter of intellectual understanding, though this is a critical component. We are called to have minds that are richly indwelt by the Word. This is what we seek: minds that are governed by the thoughts of God. Only then will our minds be strengthened by truth, sustained by the Spirit, and guarded in peace. Only as our minds are indwelt by truth will we find that our conscience is informed by truth and our hearts and wills are capable of living in truth.

All disciplines of the spiritual life are designed to foster the renewal of the mind, but some of them are more directly and immediately linked with this element of a Christian spirituality. There are three that stand out: Bible reading, memorization, and study. The first is the reading and study of the Bible. It is the Bible that gives the Christian believer the capacity to think and live in the light of the person and work of Christ. The ideal would be to establish a pattern of Bible reading and memorization, reading Scripture as God's Word daily with care, conscious that the original meaning of the text is largely determined by the context.

Another particularly valuable practice is to take a two- to three-hour period for extended reading. Christians often misuse the Bible by building up their knowledge of Scripture around verses and phrases rather than broader portions. Rarely do we read an individual epistle in one sitting, as it was written. We draw new insight when we read a gospel in one sitting, and we appreciate the dramatic growth of the early church as we read the book of Acts, again in one sitting. Many Christians commend the practice of reading through the Bible regularly; some have suggested reading the Scripture from Genesis through Revelation at least once every five years.

Christians of all ages have also commended the practice of Scripture *memorization*. Start with a little, perhaps, but begin. A verse a day is a place to start, but build on this. There is probably no spiritual discipline that so effectively leads to the indwelling of the mind with the Word of Christ as the practice of consistent memorization.

Another discipline directed specifically to the renewal of the mind is *study*: disciplined reflection that applies biblical truth to life. We passionately seek the truth with the confidence that we cannot know freedom unless we know truth. Our longing is for our minds to know, understand, and live according to the truth. In this respect, study is a spiritual discipline.

There are two simple but complementary steps in study. The first is acquisition of the facts. The second is reflection on the facts and their interrelationship or correlation. "What do the facts mean?" "What significance do they have?" We interpret the facts in terms of our own experience and in light of our previous study. Both steps are essential for the study to have spiritual benefit. Our study can and needs to lead us into the truth in each dimension of our lives.

As Christians we should constantly explore the full range of Christian doctrine, deepening our appreciation of the faith. Next, we need to study the faith with specific reference to our vocation. For instance, the doctor is particularly concerned with the relationship between his faith and his medical practice; the teacher seeks a biblical understanding of the student as a learner and of the task of communicating truth. Finally, all Christians need to stretch their minds to appreciate the implications of divine revelation for life, or ethics. For example, what does the Word say and mean for a father or husband? Or, for the citizen, what does the Word say about the Christian in the world?

Fortunately, in the task of study we are not alone. We stand within a community of faith. And the church has wonderful resources: scholars, teachers, writers, and preachers, who are able guides as we seek to understand and live the truth. In time we come to identify authors who are particularly helpful in the task of searching for the truth.

The goal remains always the same: we are seeking to live lives on earth consistent with the kingdom ideals and purposes of Christ. We want to think Christianly so that we can live Christianly. Our study of truth is never an end in itself; it is study that enables us to open our hearts and minds to the transforming work of God in our lives.

THE ATTITUDE OF THE HEART

Thinking Christianly is not merely a matter of knowing and understanding the truth—or even of seeing things in light of the person of Christ. A Christian mind is necessarily informed by two crucial *attitudes:* humility and gratitude. Growth in faith is dependent on growth in humility and growth in gratitude. These are the marks of a spirituality rooted in Christ: in the Incarnation, the Cross, and the Resurrection.

Ultimately, an authentic spirituality is dependent not so much on our behavior as on the posture of our hearts. Behavior, in other words, is important and is a vital indicator of the quality of our spiritual lives. But it also is derivative of a heart oriented toward God. As Paul puts it in 1 Corinthians 8, knowledge merely puffs up; it has no value apart from love. Similarly, without humility and gratitude, our understanding—our encounter with truth—will merely puff up. It will not edify. It will not renew the mind. Without humility we might have knowledge, but not wisdom; without humility, our understanding will not inform our hearts and minds in such a way that we can truly say that we are growing in faith, hope, and love.

The concept of humility may be difficult to grasp, yet this grace is so vital to Christian experience that we must stretch our thinking and seek understanding. Toward God, humility is an awareness that we are creatures dependent on God as creator and sustainer of all of life. But more, it is a growing recognition that we come before God empty-handed, as captured ably in the well-known hymn "Just as I Am." We have nothing with which to impress God or require Him to bless us. We are creatures before a transcendent, holy God. We are sinners who only know life because we live under His mercy. Humility is simply living in the truth—recognizing the reality and character of God and living in personal dependence on God as Creator and Savior.

However, humility also has a social dimension: how we see ourselves within human community. We rightly recognize the foolishness of the arrogant man who thinks he is more clever than anyone else. But Dag Hammarskjöld has noted that humility is just as much opposed to self-abasement as it is to self-exaltation. To be humble is to refuse to make comparisons.[6] Rather, in sober judgment of ourselves and of the task at hand, we are freed from the temptation to consider whether we are bigger or smaller, better or worse.

We can engage the task we are called to do without the bondage of making comparisons. This means that we are now freed from the crushing blow of criticism and from the headiness of flattery. We still hear criticism and praise, but in humility we no longer crave the one and fear the other. We can accept both gracefully. Thus Thomas Merton concludes that it is impossible to overestimate the value of true humility and its power in the Christian life.[7] In humility there is freedom — freedom from the desire for acknowledgment, praise, and vindication (the desire to be proven right).

Something must be stressed, though. Many think that humility comes with the breaking of the will; many Christian communities actively call for and encourage the idea that we are only humble when we are "broken." True spirituality, it is thought, is the human person with a defeated will. However, that is not the whole story. We must affirm that humility comes when we bow the knee and accept the liberating authority of Christ. Yet it is just as crucial that we affirm that humility comes through affirmation, blessing, and encouragement. Indeed, nothing may be so graciously humbling as the experience of receiving blessing. And many never know this. They live always with the assumption that their will is evil and contrary to God; yet the call to humility includes precisely the reality that blessing is the empowering of the human will, enabling us to eagerly seek to live in alignment with God's call on our lives.

With humility we must also speak of gratitude. The call to gratitude is one of the central exhortations of Scripture—a call to thanksgiving in all circumstances. It is a sign of humility, yet it is also the spiritual discipline that gives birth to and nurtures humility. As a teenager, I was probably rather typical of other young people who grow up in Christian homes. I was skeptical about religious faith. It seemed to me that religion was a good thing, but that it should not be overdone. I thought that Christianity was true but that it should be taken in small doses. One day, when we arrived home from a family holiday, my mother uttered a statement as we pulled into the driveway that was her typical declaration on that kind of occasion: "Thank you, Lord, for a safe trip."

Well, I decided it was time to state my case. I asked my mother why she thought we had some kind of special dispensation over our car when thousands had been on that road traveling safely. I wondered aloud why we should think that we had some kind of special treatment from God and that for some reason God was caring particularly for us. I vividly remember her response: "Gordon, all of us travel under the mercy of God. The difference is that the Christian knows this, acknowledges it, and gives thanks." The difference, I now know, is one of living in the truth. And gratitude cannot be overdone.

In turning away from sin, we turn from a lack of gratitude to an attitude of thanksgiving. Then we can grow in our gratitude until it permeates every dimension of our lives (Colossians 3:15-17). Indeed, there is a direct correspondence between the depth of our gratitude and the strength and vitality of our spiritual lives. It is out of character for us to grumble, complain, or worry. Our deep need is to grow in joyful contentment. Without growth in gratitude, our spirituality will be crippled and our task in the world will not bear fruit. Ingratitude is a sign of proud discontent, evidence that we think we deserve more. This ingratitude is pride, and it stifles life, joy, and peace.

In contrast, gratitude renews the human spirit and breathes life into our inward beings. However, we don't give thanks just because it is good for mental health. We give thanks because we recognize the goodness and mercy of God. This is found, centrally, in the reality of the Cross and the gift of life appropriated for us in Christ's death. In Christ—through nothing of ourselves—we have been chosen as God's children and have received His gift of life.

But there is more. In Christ our eyes are opened to see the reality of God's grace in even the most difficult situation. The blinders have been removed from our eyes so we can now see a hand of mercy in the midst of the deepest wrong and can recognize God's goodness in the midst of a predicament.

Notice the inherent distinction here. We do not give thanks *for* evil and difficult circumstances. Rather, our eyes have been opened to the reality of divine grace in the midst of difficulty, injustice, and even suffering. Consequently, gratitude reflects a decision to receive this grace of God—to see His mercy and goodness. Eventually this way of "seeing" can become a habit of the heart—a hallmark of our lives. As such it will become central to our spirituality and our maturation as Christian believers. Both humility and gratitude are the personal attitudes that accompany and foster true understanding—the renewal of the mind.

PERSONAL ENCOUNTER
WITH GOD

A second component of an authentic Christian spirituality is a pattern of formal prayer and worship. This is probably the component most often associated with the spiritual life. Some may even conclude that being Christian means being like everyone else except that a Christian adds *religious* activities to the daily schedule—notably prayer and worship. This is not an accurate perception, of course. True spirituality involves much more than religious activities. Nevertheless, prayer and worship are central and pivotal to an authentic spirituality. If we are going to serve God in the demanding and difficult setting to which He has called us, we can be satisfied with nothing less than a consistent and authentic encounter with God—personally in our private prayers and publicly as members of the church through the act of corporate worship.

However, it is crucial that we appreciate that when we speak of these religious activities of prayer and worship, we do so thinking in terms of a very distinctive end or purpose to them: a personal encounter with God, an encounter that fosters personal communion with the Creator.

A LIVING RELATIONSHIP

The Christian life is fundamentally a relationship with the living God. This cannot be overstated or stated too frequently. The

Christian life is a relationship with the God of Abraham and Sarah who has revealed Himself in Jesus of Nazareth. Another understanding or expression of a spiritual life may have a religious dimension, but what makes Christian spirituality distinctly Christian is precisely this reality: to be a Christian is to be in communion with Jesus Christ.

This was brought forcefully to the center of my attention through an experience I had while on a brief sabbatical leave in Wales. I was studying and writing at a small residential library in Hawarden, near the English border. While I was intent on my writing project on that Sunday afternoon, others persuaded me that I needed to take a break from my work and join them on an outing to the town of Holywell. They intended to visit an ancient Celtic well, one that for centuries has been viewed as having healing powers. I joined them, thinking a few hours away from the books might be just what I needed.

After a short bus ride we arrived in Holywell and proceeded to make our way to the famous well. However, just as we walked over the crest leading down to the well, we came upon a large procession coming from the right, heading the same way. We surmised that they were going to the well, and I suggested that perhaps we would have to come back another day. However, one member of our group promptly announced that she was joining the procession and that the rest of us might as well join in. The rest all agreed, and without further discussion we waited for an opportune time and stepped in.

Now we were heading down the road immediately ahead of a large group of Filipina nannies who were working in Wales— devout Roman Catholics and, more to the point, devout in their loyalty to Mary. They were singing the *Ave Maria*. As we walked along I certainly felt out of place. This had not been what I had expected when I headed out that afternoon; I had never been part of a procession of this kind.

Indeed, I was "out of place," and this was reinforced as we came around the bend in the road. To my amazement there was a crowd on both sides of the road denouncing our procession, condemning us, and shouting at the tops of their voices. I was shocked by the harshness of their condemnation. Clearly the object of their anger was Marian devotion. I had never before or since, though, seen such an overwhelming expression of condemnation of one Christian group by another.

One side of me wanted to protest to these angry folk along the road that I was *not* actually part of the procession; I just happened along! On the other hand, I was certainly not about to identify myself with this group shouting their condemnation upon us. It was one of those moments, which we all feel from time to time, when we are caught betwixt and between, feeling lost, rootless, and disconnected, and wondering whether we belong or even if we belong anywhere.

Well, I stayed with the procession, and together we moved into a small meadow before the large building that housed the well. This, as it turned out, was the annual procession in which the well was "opened." As a group, we made our way to the back of the crowd, keeping our distance from those now outside the fence, who continued to rain their verbal violence down upon us. As we milled about, the women handed out song sheets, and in a short time the singing began. I hope I never forget the moment we began to sing that day as we were led in the piece known as *St. Patrick's Breastplate:*

> *Christ beside me,*
> *Christ before me,*
> *Christ behind me, king of my heart*
> *Christ within me,*
> *Christ below me,*
> *Christ above me, never to part*

And the hymn goes on to speak of Christ on the right and on the left, all around us, "shield in the strife," Christ who is present to us in our sleeping and in our rising as "light of our lives."

As we sang, I was moved by the reminder that this is the heart and soul of what it means to be a Christian. Many times we are faced with an experience or a set of circumstances that threatens the stability or serenity of our lives. We lose a sense of perspective, balance, and alignment. And of course, these are those times in which we come to the reaffirmation of what really matters, what really counts for us. We are called back to the simple yet crucial reality that in the end the only thing that matters is our relationship with Jesus. And this relationship is not something we sustain but which is present to us by the Spirit. Christ is with us; Christ is before us; Christ is all around us.

But we will not appreciate this if we do not sustain—both in understanding and in practice—the conviction that the Christian life is a relationship between the triune God and His people, the church, made possible by the death of Jesus on the cross. Thus any true spirituality will necessarily take account of this reality and foster this relationship as the very heart of what it means to be a Christian.

There are at least three alternatives to this central relationship that need to be identified, recognized as false alternatives, and intentionally set aside: elevating to the center of the Christian life (1) the Bible, (2) the local church, or (3) a cause or a people. First, there is the spirituality of biblicism. Biblicism is the posture that basically views the Christian faith as the religion of the book. Under this view, the whole of the Christian life is lived in defense of and in orientation to the Bible. While the Bible is surely the Word of God and the source of life-giving and life-sustaining truth, it is imperative that we appreciate that in actual fact Scripture enables us to see, know, and serve Jesus. The Christian faith is not, in the end, about a relationship with a book; it is rather about a relationship with Jesus. We can and must affirm the authority and trustworthiness of Scripture, but precisely as the means by which we know and are kept in relationship with Jesus. The Bible is not an end in itself.

Then second, there are those whose approach to Christian spirituality is one in which the local church is the center and focus of the Christian life. Under this view, Christians are often judged by their level of participation in congregational life. A person is judged to be a good Christian if they are "active" in their local church. Again, however, this orientation is misplaced. The church is surely an essential element in Christian spirituality. We certainly are called to live in mutual submission to one another. We are called to serve one another as members of the community of faith. However, a local-church-centered spirituality assumes that somehow the church can be the pivot and center of the spiritual life. Again, such a posture implies that the church is an end rather than affirming that the church is a means to an end: to foster our individual and common identity in relationship with Jesus.

Third, we could say much the same in response to those who suggest that the Christian life is about identifying with a cause or with a people, such as those who suggest that the heart of our Christian identity is our participation in Christian mission or our willingness to stand with the poor and oppressed. Again, while such a cause or purpose is not only noble but actually integral to Christian identity, our participation in mission and our identification with the poor is an expression of our relationship with Christ. For an authentically Christian spirituality, Christ Jesus must necessarily remain as the heart and soul of who we are, what we seek, what we long for, and whom we serve.

The Mystical Dimension of the Christian Life

But this poses a problem. Our understanding of personal relationships has many dimensions. We have wife–husband, mother–child, teacher–student, colleague–colleague, and a wide variety of other relationships in our daily lives. It is probably easy for us to picture these kinds of relationships in our minds. We can imagine the contexts and behavior patterns and picture specific persons who have these relationships with us. Even the most imaginative person, however, would struggle to envision a relationship with someone whom we cannot see, hear, or touch.

How do we maintain and nurture a relationship with a majestic, holy, and mysterious God? Yes, we know from the New Testament that we only have a relationship with God through Jesus Christ. But Christ is now the ascended Lord! He resides in another sphere of reality. How does one have a relationship—a meaningful communion—with the cosmic Lord of the universe?

This sounds like an absurd question to many Christians. They probably have lived with the reality of God as part of their common speech. God has always been there and a relationship with this one named God is something they have never questioned. But think of it. Is it not amazing that common, sinful people can enjoy a relationship of joy, love, and even collegiality (did He not call us coworkers?) with the God who made the heavens and the earth? We cannot take it for granted.

Because we are creatures and also sinners, our relationship with God is one that cannot be presumed upon. Further, modern urban life is not conducive to the spiritual life. Often our casual assumption of God's accessibility and availability is a sign that our relationship with Him lacks vitality and depth. We must recognize that this relationship is one that crosses two spheres of existence: nature and supranature. It is a *mystical* relationship in that it transcends the material world.

Some may wonder at the use of the word "mystical." However, it is precisely the right word when we want to speak of a relationship between humanity and the Creator of humanity, a relationship that is sustained with One whom we cannot see, cannot touch, and cannot hear (at least in terms of audible voice). It is a relationship that though sustained by the senses, surely transcends the senses. As we read in 1 Peter 1:8, we have a relationship with One whom we cannot see, but who by faith we believe is there and hears us, loves us, and sustains us.

It is astonishing that the living God actually seeks those who would worship Him in spirit and in truth. This same God invites us to His banquet table. Our Creator welcomes all who are hungry and thirsty and who willingly respond to the emptiness in their hearts with a rejection of sin and a trust in the only One who can fill the void. But the relationship is still a mystical one, and like all relationships it requires care, thoughtfulness, and spiritual discipline if it is to be sustained and strengthened. In the goodness of God we have a wealth of resources — the words of Scripture and the devotional writings from the church's history. We are not alone in our quest.

New Testament Images of the Christian Life

As we seek to comprehend the character of the Christian life and the relationship we are called to have with God, the Scriptures, of course, are our primary guide. Through the Old and New Testaments, God has provided a variety of images, or pictures, to help us understand who He is and how we can know, love, and serve Him. Also, in examining our Christian heritage, we can discern how our spiritual forefathers and mothers were able to maintain a relationship with the God of the Bible. We are not the first to attempt what may seem overwhelming: a personal relationship with the creator God.

The Bible helps us through picture language to understand what it means to be a Christian. Hundreds of images taken from all dimensions of human life serve as windows into the reality of God and what it means to be in a relationship with Him. Three of these images, I believe, are central to the New Testament, particularly in the epistles of Paul: the spiritual child, union with Christ, and walking in the Spirit. They portray the mystical dimension of the Christian life.

First, this relationship is portrayed as one between father and child. God sent His Son so we might all have a relationship with the Father. We are no longer estranged from the One who made us (Galatians 4:4-6). This was the mission of God, His very purpose in revealing Himself through the incarnate Christ. God, in Christ, was seeking to restore orphaned men and women to a relationship of a spiritual child. We are children to a Father. The unique sonship of Jesus is the model for the maturing childlikeness (the redeemed child) that we enter by becoming disciples of Jesus. Through His death, Jesus makes it possible for us to be children of the Father, and in His life He exhibits what that relationship means. We are children of our Father by virtue of His indwelling Spirit. It is by the Spirit that we have an inner assurance of our identity as children of the Father, and it is by the Spirit that we can know our Father intimately and maintain a relationship of love with Him.

Though the Christian life is fundamentally a mystical relationship with God, it also has a visible dimension that is unavoidably linked to it: the relationship of the believer (the child) to his brothers and sisters (God's other children). John emphasizes in his first epistle that love of God is only conceivable when there is a corresponding love for fellow believers. He joyfully declares, "How great is the love the Father has lavished on us, that we should be called children of God!" (1 John 3:1, NIV). But then he is very blunt: "If anyone says, 'I love God,' yet hates his brother, he is a liar. For anyone who does not love his brother, whom he has seen, cannot love God, whom he has not seen. And he has given us this command: Whoever loves God must also love his brother" (1 John 4:20-21, NIV). Though distinct, these two dimensions of the Christian life are inseparable and mutually dependent: the solitary and the communal, love of God and love of brother, the mystical and the earthly.

The child as an image of the spiritual life is one that is being rediscovered in recent years by theologians. James Houston suggests that this image of the Christian life is particularly appropriate for the contemporary Christian in the face of secular humanism, urbanization, and the stress on secular, technological, self-confident humanity.[1] This image captures the longing of contemporary humanity. It acknowledges that as children we are dependent learners, and it affirms the principle of loyalty in a pluralistic and rapidly changing society. Houston suggests that for many the image of a spiritual child will significantly enhance their comprehension of a Christian's relationship with God.

Second, in the New Testament the Christian life is pictured as union with Christ. The believer is portrayed as one who lives in a unique bond of fellowship with the ascended Lord Jesus. Our baptism initiating us as Christian believers symbolizes our union with Christ in His death and resurrection (Romans 6:3-4). Paul speaks of this when he describes the Christian life as one of both receiving Christ and then of being rooted and built up in Him (Colossians 2:6-7). Though the apostle goes on to stress other critical aspects of the Christian life, this constitutes a simple statement of what that life is. In coming to Christian faith, we entered into a relationship with Jesus. Now, as we grow and mature in our faith, we do not move beyond that fundamental principle—the relationship with Jesus. Our commitment is to deepen and strengthen that bond.

John's gospel provides the most graphic New Testament example of this image in the well-known passage describing the vine and the branches. Union with Christ is portrayed as being grafted as a branch into a vine; we "bear much fruit" if we "abide" in Him (John 15:5). Spiritual life in a natural, material world is— somehow, in ways we can hardly comprehend—a mystical union with the ascended Lord Jesus. We can literally live in union with Christ. He is the source of our life—our emotional, spiritual, intellectual, and even physical energy. This relationship confounds the materialist, for the Christian actually sees this mystical union with Christ to be the central fact of his or her existence.

Yet we need to go a step further. The expression "union with Christ" still needs to be explained in practical terms. What does it mean not in abstract or theological language but in normal everyday life to be in union with an ascended Lord? The following formula may be helpful: true spirituality is knowing, loving, and serving Jesus.[2] Though a summary statement like this cannot capture in full what it means to be in union with Christ, it is useful as we look for ways in which to structure a spiritual life. We seek to know Jesus of Nazareth intimately. We seek to love Him ardently. We seek to serve Him wholeheartedly and effectively. In following this formula we avoid serving one whom we do not love or loving one whom we do not know. Service without love is dry and legalistic, and eventually it will lack any measure of compassion. Love without knowledge is sentimentalism. Rather, as Christians, our longing is to know Jesus, who reveals fully the God of heaven; our desire is to love Him in response to His love for us; our commitment is to serve Him and to do so effectively.

There is a certain logical progression here—we serve the one we love, the one we have come to know. Knowledge precedes love, which in turn precedes service. But it is not so simple. Actually, each of these dimensions informs and strengthens the other. Service for Christ deepens our knowledge and strengthens our love. Love frees our minds to know Him better. The three are interdependent, forming an integrated spirituality. Together they form one way of understanding what it means to be in union with Christ.

Just as the first image of the spiritual child includes the horizontal dimension of brotherly love, union with Christ cannot be solitary. Union with Christ of necessity means union with His body, the church. Consequently, true spirituality must be conceived in both personal and corporate forms. It includes community—not the community of a social club, but the community of a living, organic body of believers worshiping and serving one head, Jesus Christ. Union with Christ includes a dynamic relationship with God's people.

The third image of this relationship is that of walking in the Spirit. We are children of the Father for we have the Spirit present within us. It is by the Spirit that we cry out, "Abba, Father," inwardly assured of His love and care. We are united with Christ through the ministry of the Holy Spirit, for it is by the Spirit that we are born again to new life.

The New Testament portrays the believer in a special relationship with the Spirit of the living God. In Galatians 3:1-3 Paul asserts that we received the Spirit by believing what we heard, not by observing the law. The apostle then expresses amazement that anyone who came to faith in such a manner would attempt to reach the goal of spiritual maturity through human effort. Can this be done? His reply is an emphatic "No!" Human effort cannot maintain the Christian life and assure its maturation. In other words, Paul is warning these early Christians against the temptation of living the Christian life through willpower—the will to obey the law.

Though obedience is vital to Christian experience, freedom from sin is only possible in submission to the Holy Spirit. We are all well aware of the frustrations of trying to live the Christian life. As we look back, our road seems marked by constant failure. We are battered and bruised by our daily struggle with sin. Paul describes his own wrestling with sin in chapter 7 of his epistle to the Romans. He understood, and he knew the solution. Very simply, he calls us to walk in the Spirit: "So I say, live by the Spirit, and you will not gratify the desires of the sinful nature. . . . Since we live by the Spirit, let us keep in step with the Spirit" (Galatians 5:16,25, NIV).

These three images of the spiritual life—the spiritual child, union with Christ, and walking in the Spirit—are not three distinct relationships. Each of these images links the Christian with a person of the Holy Trinity—Father, Son, and Spirit, respectively. But this does not imply three kinds of relationships or that there is a different relationship with each member of the Trinity. Rather, our relationship with God is one. We are in fellowship with God, through Christ, by means of the inner work of the Spirit. The images found in the New Testament are merely different ways of viewing this central truth: by virtue of the saving work of God in Christ we can enter into a personal relationship with Him. We are only children of the Father by the Spirit. Similarly, union with Christ and walking in the Spirit are different ways of viewing the same reality.

This is evident when Paul unites and blends all three images in a grand description of the Christian life. We are alive, he tells us, when we are in Christ; in Christ, we are children of God, children because we have received the Spirit (Romans 8:9-11,13-16).

Yet the value of recognizing the different images is that each can reveal a distinct dimension of our relationship with God. Aspects of our relationship expressed in varied images may capture our imaginations and foster periods of spiritual growth. It is helpful to allow one of these images to be the source of inspiration and the focus of meditation at different points in our lives, while recognizing that in time we want to appreciate all images found in the New Testament. Each casts a different light on the rich and varied aspects of a relationship with the living God. It is appropriate to allow one of these images to fuel our imaginations and give focus to our thoughts, so that as we practice the spiritual disciplines we see and experience them always as nothing but a means of fostering a relationship with the triune God. And central to the disciplines of the spiritual life is that practice that most explicitly fosters this relationship: prayer.

PRAYER

Prayer is the single most convincing evidence that the Christian life has a mystical dimension. The life of prayer is a continual reflection that there is more to life than what is visible—the Christian life is about a relationship with One whom we cannot see or touch. For the great mystics of the Middle Ages—the high-water mark in Christian mysticism—it was imperative to stress that the Christian life is not about a relationship with truth, per se, with doctrine, with an abstraction, or with a cause. It is a relationship with God, who indwells both our reality and another reality. And they stressed that we only really believe this and live accordingly when we are women and men of prayer.

Prayer speaks of another reality; and for the Christian, that reality is God. The Christian life is mystical in that it is lived in terms of two realities: the visible world and God. The Christian believes that God not only exists, but that He also lives in fellowship with His creation. And the chief means of fellowship is prayer. If we neglect our prayers, then we are in essence practical atheists, who verbally confess that there is a God but whose daily practice does not give evidence of such a conviction.

Prayer is not just words directed to the Almighty; it is not just "talking to God." It is the exercise that enables us to be in personal communion with the Creator-Redeemer. Sustaining authentic Christian life is actually inconceivable apart from an established pattern of formal prayer and worship. Prayer and worship are not only an important and obvious feature of Jesus' life and ministry; every significant church leader and spiritual master throughout the history of the church confirms this component as crucial to what it means to be a Christian.

Formal prayer and worship include personal, private prayer as well as corporate and public worship. A healthy spirituality depends on *both* dimensions. For the purposes of this discussion, though, I will focus on the personal and private. This component of the Christian life is based on a simple principle: there is no growth in the spiritual life without time spent alone with God. Solitude is essential to the deepening of the interior life. It is a means of coming to an intimate knowledge of God. By faith we not only affirm the possibility of meeting God through private prayer, but we also recognize that through this encounter we become new people who are more fully able to be God's kingdom agents in the world.

The Call to Solitude

In chapter 1 of the gospel of Mark we read of an interesting encounter between Jesus and his disciples. Very early in the morning, while it was still dark, Jesus left the home He was staying in and went off to spend some time in prayer and solitude (verse 35). Peter and his companions went looking for Him. Jesus was in demand, we read. It seems the whole town was eager to find Him. He was needed—desperately needed. The disciples could hardly suppress their frustration that Jesus was not present when He was needed. "Everyone is searching for you," they announced, amazed that Jesus was so difficult to find.

In the next verses we discover two abiding features of Jesus' ministry that are the direct result of His commitment to a life of prayer in solitude. First, He does not respond to the demands and the pleas of the townspeople of Capernaum. Rather, He calmly announces that He must go to other villages to preach, for that is His calling. Second, we note in the verses that follow that Jesus is filled with compassion and reaches out to touch a desperately needy leprous man.

The evidence is clear. Jesus' strength of ministry and depth of compassion are both directly related to the consistency and vitality of His personal prayer life. He led a life that routinely included consistent and personal encounter with His heavenly Father. Formal prayer and worship were well-established habits of His early life.

Nothing guarantees that if we pray we will have a personal encounter with God. An intimate consciousness of the presence of God is sheer gift. But the testimony of our spiritual heritage and the common experience of believers of all ages, cultures, and backgrounds confirm that when men and women eagerly dispose themselves to such an encounter in prayer and worship, God is more than willing to meet them. However, the witness of our Christian heritage suggests that true prayer has two fundamental characteristics that foster this encounter: faith and humility. We are more likely to meet and know God intimately if we are women and men who have some measure of each characteristic.

The Scriptures affirm that true prayer arises from a confidence that Jesus is the ascended Lord capable of understanding our needs and responding with wisdom and power. The writer of Hebrews affirms the dual identity of Christ: He is Lord, and as the ascended One He bears the authority and the capacity to respond to our situation (4:14-16). But He is also the incarnate One who is capable of identifying with that very set of circumstances. Yet this confidence must be matched with humility, for faith without humility is presumption. Prayer is the cry of a child dependent upon a heavenly Father. True prayer no longer seeks to impress nor gets caught up with the temptation to manipulate with words (Matthew 6:5-8). We can only pray with both confidence and humility if we know that we are loved and forgiven. But the Scriptures also make it clear that we must also forgive those who have wounded us (Matthew 6:14-15). That is, true prayer is characterized by humility as well as faith.

The Form of Our Prayers

Prayer is at the heart of spiritual experience because the Christian life is mystical — a life lived in communion and dependence upon Jesus. A constant danger, though, is that we would become legalistic about the form a personal, formal prayer time should take. I remember reading a booklet early in my Christian life that suggested all committed Christians devote the first hour of the day to God. The message I got was that commitment is reflected in one's willingness to spend early-morning time in prayer — the earlier the better. Well, if I was not a committed Christian, I wanted to be, and so I began a regimen of early-morning rising, striving to stay awake, meditating on a passage of Scripture, and interceding for my needs and those of others. But it was agony. More often than not I lived in guilt because of a lack of a meaningful prayer experience. And prayer increasingly became a burden.

Later I came to realize that a better guiding rule is that we should give God the *best* time of our day; and by best I mean the hour when we are mentally alert and most capable of being present to God in our prayer. Different people have different physical and emotional metabolisms. Some individuals are more awake in the morning; others, in the late evening. Each person needs to decide for himself which time of the day is most profitable. For some, the time may need to vary because of changes in the daily schedule.

Although we cannot insist on the specific form that a personal, private time of prayer should take, the weight of our spiritual heritage supports the idea that we set aside between a half-hour and an hour. This seems both wise and reasonable. Most of us need that much time to still our minds, renew our sense of perspective, meditate meaningfully on a text of Scripture, and respond with an open heart and mind to what we sense God saying to us. We need to actively work against the idea that we are too busy for extended prayer time. Few elements of our spiritual lives will prove our mettle as much as our willingness to spend time with God.

Does it not seem strange that we sometimes act as if God has given us so much to do that we can no longer spend extended time with Him? Isn't the lack of a significant, consistent pattern of personal, formal prayer a sign that much of our work, our business, is our own doing and not the will of God? It is inconceivable to think God would give us so much to do that we can no longer spend extended time with Him. John Carmody quotes an Eastern theologian who notes, "When the devil wants to detach someone from the one thing necessary, he occupies him with a lot of work which does not leave him a free moment for meditation or for deepening his interior life."[3]

This is a strong reminder that we need to place a fence around some period in our daily schedule to meet alone with God. This applies particularly to the urban dweller. The busyness and superficiality of city life makes it particularly urgent that we establish a pattern for personal, private prayer.

We also need to find a place of quiet for an effective and consistent encounter with God. Our internal space is subtle and is surely affected by external space. Noise and confusion around us are not conducive to inner peace and reflection. We are embodied souls. For an extended time of quiet, we need space.

Not only do we need to be attentive to space; we also need form, an intentionality to our praying. There are many ways in which an hour of prayer could be structured. (See a suggested format for an hour of daily formal prayer in Appendix 1.) But the accumulated wisdom of our spiritual heritage teaches that there are three basic elements that can make prayer more fruitful: centering of thoughts, meditation on a text of Scripture, and time of communion with God.

First, it is particularly helpful to begin the hour with a conscious centering of our thoughts. Our busy minds need to be stilled; the turmoil of our hearts needs to be quieted so that we can pray. A favorite psalm or a well-known hymn can be helpful for centering; for some, a brief prayer of submission to the Spirit brings thoughts into focus and opens the mind to hear God's Word.

Second, the hour could include a time of meditation on a text of Scripture. Ideally, the text should be one in which most of the basic questions on its interpretation have already been answered. It is not too beneficial, in terms of prayer, if we meditate on a text we do not understand. Therefore, we would be wise to meditate on portions of Scripture we have studied and about which we have a basic understanding. We want to avoid the situation where we are impressed by a promise in Scripture, think that perhaps this promise might apply to us, and only later discover we had misread the text. This does not mean we can hear God speak in prayer only if we are thoroughgoing exegetes. Many have been impressed by the presence and voice of God in ways that would no doubt perplex a biblical scholar. However, we must act responsibly and appreciate that our understanding of Scripture enhances our capacity to hear God. Our prayers can and must be sustained and informed by our study of Scripture.

Third, the time in prayer needs to include the element of communion, preferably found in a time of extended silence in the presence of the Lord. The time of prayer is, literally, a time with God. We are not just in prayer in order to receive our marching orders; neither is it only a time for repentance. These elements will be a part of our prayer, but a time alone with God—an hour of solitude in our prayer closet (see Matthew 6:6)—is more than anything else a time of fellowship with God Himself. Our prayer experience is *governed* by the Word of God; the God we meet reveals Himself *through* the Scriptures. But this is not essentially, in the end, a communion with the Scriptures. It is, very simply, a time of encounter with God. As such, it is appropriate to consciously set aside our Bible and with minds informed by the Scriptures enjoy the presence of God and delight in His company.

The goal of our time with God is to come to *know* Him. Although this knowledge is grounded and immersed in the truth of Holy Scripture, the knowledge we seek is *experiential*. Our longing is to be a people who know their God—and we come to know God individually through this personal encounter in the solitude of our prayers.

Responding in Prayer

God is present to us in our prayer; and in our prayer we are called to be present to God. And thus, since God speaks to us through our meditation on Scripture, we must consider our response to God. In knowing God and hearing His Word, we choose then, out of silence, to respond. There are four classic responses: adoration, thanksgiving, confession, and care-casting. Our prayer can be a response appropriate to the text we have been meditating on and the word we have heard in our silence.

First, we can respond to God with adoration. If He reveals something about Himself that deeply impresses us, whether it is His wisdom, goodness, beauty, or power, then we need to allow our hearts to burst forth in response, allowing the fullness of our hearts to be expressed in adoration. In part we know ourselves through a recognition of what creates awe and wonder within us.

Second, our self-knowledge is enhanced through the spiritual exercise of thanksgiving. When we start reflecting on God's goodness to us, we are soon freed from a heavy spirit. Praise is most meaningful when it arises in response to God's goodness to us—as we feel and experience His mercy. Ultimately, we thank Him for His greatest gift, the life we have in Jesus Christ.

Third, self-knowledge includes confession of sin, an awareness of where we have failed in the eyes of God. Knowing God cannot help but enable us to more clearly see our own character and behavior. An awareness of His presence consistently leads us to confess we have fallen short of His ideal for us. But it is most helpful to think of our confession as a reflection of God's assessment of us. It is not so much a self-examination as it is an opening up to God for Him to reveal His purposes for us. Our question in prayer would be, God, how do you see me; where do you feel I need to grow and turn from sin? In the end, this form of confession bears the greatest fruit and has the most potential to assist us toward spiritual maturity.

Fourth, our time of prayer can include the spiritual exercise of care-casting.[4] One of our vulnerable areas in spiritual warfare is our fears or worries. There is a real sense in which our greatest fear is also our weakest point for attack by the Evil One. Conversely, in His Word, God exhorts us to cast all our cares upon Him. We are invited to place all our anxieties upon His shoulders. There is no reason for us to worry, for He is committed to caring for us. In giving Him our cares, we can know His peace, which transcends understanding (Philippians 4:6-7; 1 Peter 5:7).

Many years ago our family traveled across a section of western Canada, from Calgary, Alberta, to Kamloops, British Columbia. Our two sons were quite young at the time. We had been traveling for less than an hour out of Calgary when Micah, our youngest, asked where we would be spending the night. I told him it would be in Kamloops after six or seven hours of driving. But that did not satisfy him, and so he asked again. So I told him, "At a motel in Kamloops, Micah."

"But Dad, *which* motel?" he wanted to know.

"I do not know, son; *some* motel, *any* motel," I replied.

"But how do you know there will be a motel there?" Well, my dear son had grown up in the Philippines and did not realize, I thought, that every little town in Canada has a motel, and Kamloops, a good-size city, would have plenty of motels. But he was still not reassured. I was feeling a little frustrated with him, but I turned and said, "Micah, let me worry about this; you sit in the back, enjoy the trip. Your dad will worry about where we spend the night."

That was all he needed. He relaxed and immediately stopped bothering me. And then I saw what had happened. It was an entirely reasonable concern, this matter of where we would spend the night. But it was too big a matter for a six-year-old to be worried about. Similarly, our Father in heaven loves to receive us and hear of our deepest fears and concerns. It is not that our cares and fears are not valid. They are real areas of concern; we are worried about our well-being and the welfare of those we love. My son was concerned about where we would sleep. This was a legitimate matter for concern; it was not infantile to be worried about this. But as a child he did not need to fret. His mind was unable to handle the burden of this fundamental need for our family. Similarly, as creatures of our heavenly Father, we worry about concerns that are too big for us, and He bids us cast all of our cares upon Him. They are important matters, but His Word to us is that He will carry them (1 Peter 5:6-7).

Each of these four classic responses to the Lord in prayer may also serve as a suitable means of centering our thoughts as we begin our hour. If our minds are filled with awe in response to the beauty of God's creation, then it is appropriate to begin our prayers with adoration. We can begin with thanksgiving in response to the goodness of God. Or, if there is sin or an anxiety that is disturbing our spirit, it is essential that we resolve these concerns even as we enter our prayers, and in so doing, we will be centering our thoughts (1 John 1:9; Philippians 4:6).

Not all of these elements for responding to God need be included each day in our prayer. Rather, it is helpful to see these spiritual exercises as resources upon which we can draw as we pray. As we do, we will find that our prayer is consistently more fruitful.

Also, it is important to stress that when it comes to our personal prayers, our response to God is not generic or impersonal;

we respond individually and intentionally. It is very much *our* response. And it is most truly our response when it is congruent with who we are — when there is no pretense, no attempt to be anything but ourselves in the presence of God. Consequently, we come to discover that in prayer we come to a greater self-understanding, for we come to know ourselves and see ourselves as God sees us. Lack of self-knowledge is one of the profound effects of the Fall. Sin leads us to self-deception. In contrast, the hope of the new heavens and the new earth is that we will know fully even as we are fully known (1 Corinthians 13:12). Through our personal encounter with God in formal prayer, one of the most significant benefits of knowing God is that we come to know ourselves as well.

Discernment, Intercession, and Renewed Commitment

Our prayer thus far has strengthened our communion with God. We know God and ourselves better as a result of this encounter. Now we are prepared to focus our attention again on our world and our responsibilities. We have heard God speak to us through our meditation on Holy Scripture, and we have sought to respond in truth with adoration, thanksgiving, confession, and care-casting. But now we consider again the world into which we are called to live and serve God. We think of our relationships and how God is calling us to live with generosity, grace, and devotion — in our work, in the church, and in our homes and neighborhoods. Consequently, it is appropriate that prayer include three additional elements: *discernment*, how God is calling us to act in the world in the face of the various choices we might be facing; *intercession*, as we ask for God's grace to intervene in the world; and *renewed commitment*, as we devote ourselves to be all that God calls us to be in the world.

The first of these, discernment, is an acknowledgment that we live our days in response to God's particular call on our lives. We can anticipate the day with a heart open to what God is calling us to do that day. With openness of heart, we can ask for clarity: What is most important today? If I cannot do all I would *like* to do on this day, what most represents God's call on my life today? If there are choices I need to make, this is an opportunity to ask for God's wisdom in those choices.

Our spiritual heritage would suggest that this intentional act of discernment is enhanced through reflection on our joys and sorrows. This may seem strange to many. What do our feelings have to do with prayer? Many of us were actually taught to deny feelings, to live without reference to our emotions (at least intentionally). But the human person is an emotional being. Therefore, recognition of our feelings is a crucial factor in self-understanding. It is also a key means by which we can appreciate how God is working in our lives.[5] In reflecting on the touchstones of our lives—our joys and sorrows—we can mature in the art of spiritual discernment. It is helpful to work with a journal and to look back on our prayers, noting especially the feelings experienced in the times of silence following the meditation upon the Word. Naturally, this takes time. It takes a commitment not merely to prayer, but to extended prayer—time alone with God.

Our daily prayers should also include intercession for our needs and the needs of others. Our Father delights to hear and respond to the needs of His children. Further, one of the pivotal means by which we serve others is through our intercession. For many Christians, prayer is *equated* with intercession. In stressing the need to see prayer as communion, I am not denying the place of petition in prayer. To the contrary, intercession is a key component of our prayer. But many have found that in emphasizing communion and discernment in prayer, our time of intercession is not so long. It may well be that this development reflects a greater knowledge of God and a keener sensitivity to His will. If our intercession arises out of our communion with God, then it follows that we will intercede with a deeper appreciation of God's work in the world and in the lives of others. And I have found that my prayers are simpler (not simplistic, just more simple) when they are first and foremost the fostering of communion with God. I can intercede with greater confidence and more peace, with less anxiety, and with less inclination to either complain to God or be impatient with God.

Finally, it is vital that our prayers conclude with a fresh commitment to the Lord. If we have confessed sin, our commitment is to turn from sin; if we have cast our cares on our Father, then our commitment is to trust Him more; if we have heard His call to serve Him, then our commitment is one of simple obedience. This includes the conscious dependence upon the grace of God for that to which He is calling us.

THE SPIRITUAL RETREAT

A regular time in prayer was a consistent part of Jesus' experience. But there is also evidence that on occasion He spent a more extended time apart from the crowds and needy people—sometimes alone and sometimes with His disciples. For example, Jesus' initial ministry began only after an extended time in retreat—the remarkable experience of forty days in the desert.

The example of Jesus is a reminder of the consistent word we hear through the writings of our spiritual forefathers and mothers: there is significant value not only in a daily time of prayer, but also in a spiritual retreat. At regular intervals in our lives—particularly at crucial turning points or decision-making times—it is valuable if not essential that we take an extended time to be with God. This could be a retreat of a day or several days. Fruitful as our daily time of prayer may be, we often recognize that the intense activity and heaviness of our daily lives and responsibilities require extended time away from them. We need a renewal of perspective, a fresh sense of the love and goodness of God, and wisdom in the face of a critical decision.

In many respects, a spiritual retreat can follow the pattern of our daily prayers. The same components and exercises can be used in a more extensive and thorough fashion in a retreat. (A suggested format for a spiritual retreat has been provided in Appendix 2.) But there are factors that could make a retreat different from our daily prayers in more ways than just the length of our time with God.

Ideally, a prayer retreat should include the element of spiritual direction. If possible, there should be an individual who can serve as a guide in our prayer lives, someone who can help us interpret our prayer experience, encourage us to persevere when we are discouraged, and serve as a co-discerner in a time of decision making. More will be said about the possible role of a spiritual director in a later chapter.

Also, a spiritual retreat can serve as an opportunity for us to grow in wisdom and spiritual discernment (in a sense different from our daily prayers). At turning points in our lives, we need to seek the mind of God and allow His redeeming presence to purify our motives and clarify our vision of what God is doing in our lives. An extended time with God is also a time of discernment.

We recognize that even with a consistent prayer life, with daily prayers that are rewarding and sustaining, we still live on the surface. For many Christians, the concerns and burdens of daily life are heavy and dominate their thinking. They will need a day or two away from their responsibilities before they can be freed of anxieties and experience an abiding peace that allows them to hear the voice of God. The busyness of our minds is not eased in a few minutes. It often takes time—extended time alone with God—before we are still enough to hear His voice and discern His perfect will for our lives.

For many of us it is only during extended time with God that we confront the deeper questions in our lives—our fears and loneliness, our pride and longing for recognition and honor, our secret sins, and our lack of devotion to Christ.

As with daily prayers, the spiritual retreat is governed by a simple principle: we seek to know and love Christ more fully. We believe we can meet Him in quietness and solitude. It is not that

Christ is not everywhere present by His Spirit; it is not that the Lord is only to be found in our prayer closet. Not at all. It is simply that if we are going to meet God and hear His voice and grow in wisdom as we meet and encounter our Lord, we need first to still our hearts and minds. Every day we need to step aside from the business of our daily responsibilities for personal and private prayer. But then, perhaps every few months or at least once a year we need to step back from the demands of our lives and our work for a more extended time of prayer. For example, many have found it possible and immensely valuable to take one day every six weeks for an extended time of prayer. Yet others make it a point and practice to have an annual extended retreat of several days duration. And consistently what we find is that in this extended time of retreat the experience of prayer itself is deepened and we grow in our understanding, our capacity to be discerning people, and our ability to act with integrity in a way that can hardly happen if we depend solely on a daily time of prayer. The retreat, then, becomes the complement to our daily prayers.

Finally, it is worth noting that our daily, private prayers and our spiritual retreats complement our participation in public worship with the people of God. In fact, even when we pray "alone," we are always praying with the whole company of God's people as prayer unites us with the church in heaven and on earth.

VOCATION AND CHRISTIAN SERVICE

Spirituality encompasses the whole of life. One of the classic, though very common, errors concerning the Christian life is the idea that "spirituality" refers to religious activities. Many think of their lives as having secular and sacred dimensions; often, for them the sacred or spiritual concerns their religious activities.

The truth of this is that our prayer is the heart or core of our spirituality. However, true spirituality includes *every* aspect of life. It is as whole beings that we are children of the Father; our identity as Christians intersects every dimension of our lives. We are in union with Christ and walking in the Spirit every day, regardless of whether we are at work, at play, in prayer, or asleep. Regardless of our roles or occupations, our work or activity in the world is a vital element of an authentic spirituality.

As we develop a viable spirituality that will enable us to know the grace of God, we will see that a true spiritual model must account for the fact that we live in a real, concrete, tangible world. True spirituality is not otherworldly; rather, it enables us to be fully in the world. In His prayer recorded in John 17, Jesus Himself explicitly says that He is not asking that we be taken out of the world. His prayer, instead, is that we would be made holy as we live in the world. All authentic models of spirituality will take this dimension into account.

The incarnation of Christ gloriously affirms that the Christian life is mystical in that it is lived in connection with the transcendent, the living God. But the Incarnation is also a tremendous affirmation that true spirituality is an *earthly* reality. Jesus Himself took on flesh and in so doing declared not only that the world was created by God, but also that His redemption takes place in space and time in the created order.

This can be confusing at times. We recognize that we are of this world, but we also see clearly that our identity as Christians is far removed from the values of contemporary society. We know that we are citizens of this world, but we are also convinced that our home is with the Father in heaven.

The New Testament provides us with powerful images for the mystical dimension of a Christian spirituality: we are children of the Father, in union with Christ, and walking in the Spirit. In other words, even as the New Testament graciously provides us with images of the mystical dimension of the Christian life, it also provides us with a central image that captures the meaning of the earthly dimension of our spiritual existence. We find this principally in the announcement and teaching of Jesus concerning the kingdom of God. We cannot begin to live with grace and integrity unless we see this world and respond to it in light of the reign of Christ. The Christian life finds meaning and purpose because it is life lived under the kingdom rule of God. This recognition is essential if we are to fully appreciate our relationship to the world and to understand what it means to fulfill our vocations within diverse social contexts.

THE KINGDOM AND THE CHRISTIAN

The Scriptures emphasize that the eternal plan of God is to reconcile all things to Himself and to one another. This divine purpose is identified as the kingdom or reign of God. God's purpose is to establish His kingdom in and through human history. And He does this through His Son, Jesus Christ, such that the kingdom is found in Jesus Christ—it is embodied in His presence and His rule. To live in the kingdom of God is to choose to live under the authority— the life-giving rule—of Jesus of Nazareth. Jesus came announcing the kingdom. His evangelism was to proclaim the fulfillment of the kingdom in Himself and to invite men and women to repent and live under His kingdom rule. Hence, to be a Christian is to live under the dynamic rule of Christ. The goal of our salvation is to live under the reign of Christ in the world in every aspect of life.

But there is more to this idea of God's kingdom. In announcing the presence of the kingdom clearly, Jesus implies that His kingdom is not merely a matter of individual responses to His invitation. He is proclaiming His Messianic identity and right to rule over all things—over the whole created order. Paul affirms that the mission of God in Christ is not merely to redeem a few individuals here and there, but to reconcile *all things* in heaven and on earth to Himself. But this reconciliation is possible only insofar as Christ is Lord. In the writings of Paul we read,

> And [God] made known to us the mystery of his will according-ing to his good pleasure, which he purposed in Christ, to be put into effect when the times will have reached their fulfill-ment—to bring all things in heaven and on earth together under one head, even Christ. (Ephesians 1:9-10, NIV)

> For God was pleased to have all his fullness dwell in him, and through him to reconcile to himself all things, whether things on earth or things in heaven, by making peace through his blood, shed on the cross. (Colossians 1:19-20, NIV)

This is tremendous news! It is exhilarating to think that in and through Christ Jesus, God is bringing peace between Himself and the whole created order. It is no wonder, then, that we read in the eighth chapter of Paul's epistle to the Romans that the whole creation is groaning in anticipation of our full redemption as the children of God (8:19).

We need, though, to add a cautionary but critical note. Jesus, as King, has come and has announced the kingdom, and so the kingdom of God is present now just as Jesus is present. His presence is the essence of the kingdom. But Jesus has yet to come in His full glory and power to consummate His kingdom and bring justice and peace to every corner of the universe. In the coming of Jesus in the Incarnation, His kingdom was *fulfilled*, but it is yet to be *consummated*. This distinction is critical. The kingdom of God is present, but so is the kingdom of darkness. Jesus came and announced that God's kingdom is at hand, but the victory over the forces of evil is not yet complete.

The reality of the kingdom that is present but not yet consummated gives us patience to let God do His work in His time; we know that all is not yet as it will be, but just as surely we know that it will come. For example, I know that the reality of the kingdom has engaged my life and that through Jesus Christ I have a new identity, a new purpose, and a new orientation in my work and my relationships. However, I also just as surely know I am not yet all I hope to be. God's salvation is both past tense (we have known His saving grace) and future tense (we look forward to the day of our salvation).

Further, patience with the coming of the kingdom means we graciously accept that we live in a broken world. The image and motif of the kingdom call us to appreciate that we still experience this brokenness, that death is part of life in this world, that suffering, setback, and disappointment are part of what it means to live in the kingdom that is *present* but not yet *fulfilled*. It means that our lives in the world will have times of great joy — indicators of God's kingdom, signs that the kingdom has come and that it will come. But we just as surely experience the dark side of this broken world — indicators that the kingdom has not yet been consummated. For many, this call to patience is the most difficult challenge of the Christian life — the call to wait for God to do His work in His time. And at times the only thing we have is our faith, our deep conviction that despite all the evidence — for we surely live in a broken world—God is on the throne of the universe; His kingdom has come and will yet come.

The image of the kingdom, then, reminds us that a believer lives in a dynamic tension. The Christian engages two worlds, two realities at the same time. We are citizens of both earth and heaven, and until the final consummation of the kingdom when earth and heaven are one, we live constantly in the midst of spiritual warfare. This warfare is both an inner reality (the battle for our minds) and an external battle (for justice and peace in the social structures of our world). The latter is a battle for Christian priorities and values as distinctive in society—our cultural, social, and political identity. The former is the believer's own battle for a renewed mind. Naturally, the two spheres are linked. God's kingdom rule in our society is highly dependent on His kingdom rule in our minds. But the renewal of our minds is not possible if we ignore social, intellectual, and economic issues. The two spheres are mutually dependent.

Lack of appreciation for the kingdom will consistently lead to a warped spirituality. In some cases it has led to a wholly inward and individual spirituality that ignores social and economic injustices as well as the predicament of a neighbor who has not heard the gospel. The loss of kingdom awareness has led some to an uncritical acceptance of social and cultural perspectives, so that Christianity has been identified with political movements or cultural ideals. Ultimately the gospel suffers.

But a recovery of the centrality of this motif can give the Christian community a vitally needed perspective on the world. If we are to have an authentic spirituality in the world, we need to recover a vision of the Christian life that encompasses all of creation—that of the kingdom of God. Viewed from another perspective, a recovery of the centrality of the kingdom to a Christian spirituality will help the Christian community recover unity in the Christian life. We struggle to make sense of the different elements of our lives; we all have a deep underlying longing to find some kind of cohesion or integrity to our fragmented human experience. All of us feel this fragmentation on some level. For one it might be the attempt to make sense of his life as a father, doctor, church deacon, and husband. And he wonders, What is the focus, the unifying principle that brings all these roles together? For another, her concern may be to make some sense of the fact that life moves between both the private and public, between times of solitude and times of community, times of personal struggle and times when she feels the burden of social oppression. We have this longing to make sense of it all, to see and hold on to the big picture—something that can keep the fragmented character of our lives from pulling us apart.

The image of the kingdom can effectively serve as that unifying principle when it complements the mystical-relational images presented in the previous chapter. Through the image of the kingdom we recognize that spirituality can no longer be viewed as merely touching upon the religious dimensions of our lives. Suddenly, the spiritual is not just what I do in my prayer closet or with fellow believers during public worship. True spirituality is kingdom living, which of necessity means that we can see God in the whole of our lives, in private and public, at work and in the home, in the church and in the street, and even at play—whether with children or in sports activities or in some form of healthy entertainment. The kingdom becomes the unifying or umbrella principle that brings together every dimension of our lives.

Consequently, we are freed from the oppressive burden that religious activities are somehow more important than domestic activities and work. If all that we are and do comes under the kingdom, then religious activities are surely important. But not all life is religion! We are members of families. We have occupations and responsibilities in our places of work. We have leisure time to enjoy friends, hobbies, and the arts. If we deny or undermine the other dimensions of our lives, we subtly ignore the centrality of the kingdom in God's redemptive plan. It means that my work at the office is just as important as my participation in worship; both are lived under the reign of Christ Jesus. The whole of our lives—each dimension—is lived in terms of the kingdom and therefore is an aspect of our spirituality. True spirituality is the whole of life lived in relationship with the divine Trinity—a mystical relationship. It is also the whole of life lived in the world under the kingdom rule of God.

GOD'S WORK AND OUR WORK

If our life in the world is going to be an integrated and sustaining element in our spiritual life, it requires that we think Christianly about *God's* work in the world (the image of the kingdom) but also about our work in the world. God's work is that of establishing His kingdom; and this is our prayer, that His will would be done on earth as it is in heaven. However, the appreciation of God's work by definition means that we have a radically different perspective on our own work, on our activity, whether it be in the world, in the church, or within the context of house and home. To appreciate this, we need to recover a biblical understanding of work itself and then of vocation.

When we think about life in terms of the kingdom, we are seeking to make sense of life as it was originally created to be. This means that we embrace afresh the reality that in creation, humanity was given work to do. The first man and the first woman were both charged with the wonder of *working*—of engaging God's creation and making a difference in that creation. For the parents of humanity, this work was that of naming the animals and tilling the earth (Genesis 1:29; 2:19). With sin, however, this work became *toil* (Genesis 3:17-18). Yet the principle remains: we were created to work. To be human is to be created in the image of God, who creates and calls us to re-create. God gives us skill, ability, and talent; in the same way He gives us a love of working with our minds and with our hands in such a way that we actually make a difference.

Most of us long for this, though for some the desire for work has been dulled in ways that should cause us to ache for them.

When people are lazy, they are missing out on the joy of being human. We were created to work and to find joy, satisfaction, and even pleasure in our work.

However, as already noted, with sin in the world, our work, while it will certainly at times bring us joy and satisfaction, will just as surely be a source of pain and discouragement to us, for as we've stressed, the kingdom has come, but it has not yet been consummated. One day, when Jesus makes all things well, our work will be one of pure joy. But as we live on this side of that day, we do so recognizing that work is both joy and toil. The implications are enormous.

First, this means that we take our work seriously. Our work is not something that interferes with genuine spirituality; it is integral to what it means to be a Christian. For so many Christian communities, there is the implicit assumption (sometimes an *explicit* assumption) that prayer is superior to work. I notice this, for example, when I am working on a project with a committee and someone suggests that rather than "working" so much we should spend more time praying about our work. While prayer is certainly vital to the work of a committee, it is often portrayed as a superior activity to work. We are, though, called to both prayer *and* work. If we are consumed with our work and neglect our prayers, then we have lost a true spirituality; but just as surely, we have lost our way if we are consumed with prayer and neglect our work in all of our diverse duties and responsibilities. Both prayer and work are vital to a genuinely Christian spirituality. As Dietrich Bonhoeffer put it so well, "Prayer should not be hindered by work, but neither should work be hindered by prayer. . . . Prayer is entitled to its time. But the bulk of the day belongs to work. . . . Without the burden and labor of the day, prayer is not prayer, and without prayer, work is not work."[1]

Second, this also means we affirm that work in the world is a vital expression and element of a Christian spirituality. Many who affirm the value of work still make a distinction between religious work and work that some call "secular." However, in the full affirmation of the place of work in human life and identity, we refuse to make this distinction. Both have their place in the lives of those who seek to love and serve Jesus Christ. The work of the carpenter is equally as sacred and honorable as that of the preacher or religious teacher. And for the lay person who is called to be a dentist or a banker, the actual work in the bank or the dentist office is good work, and we must not think that such people use their time better if they are also involved in teaching a Sunday School class, that they are more spiritual people if they are actively involved in their local church. Indeed, it may well be the case that if a dentist neglects her practice while serving the church, she is not faithful to the work to which she is called.

A. W. Tozer actually suggests that the Devil is bent on persuading Christians that their work in the world is of less value than their religious duties; it is the Devil who would "remind the Christian that he is giving the better part of his day to the things of this world and allotting to his religious duties only a trifling portion of his time . . . and unless great care is taken, this will create confusion and bring discouragement and heaviness of heart."[2]

Third, in this affirmation of work we also need to affirm and celebrate the work of those who make a house a home and in so doing raise children and spend their days responding to the needs of children. The work of a homemaker is not second-class work to those who have a career in the world. Indeed, Proverbs 31 celebrates equally the person who is a domestic as much as the one who is a merchant buying and selling in the marketplace.

Finally, to celebrate work is to affirm those who work with minds, in the world of ideas in teaching and learning, as well as those who work with their hands, in professions, in management and administration, in the trades, or as laborers in agricultural fields. While some societies and cultures might affirm some forms of work as more noble, for the Christian all work is good and noble, and carries with it an inherent dignity.

Work, then, is a gift from God. While we recognize that work becomes toil due to sin, it is still a gift from God. It is worth doing and worth doing well. As Christians we can celebrate work as a gift and not bemoan having to work well, or seek for a day when we can retire from work and live a life of leisure. Such thinking is antithetical to Christian spirituality. Rather, while there may be a time to retire from a career or occupation, such a transition is merely an opportunity to engage work that is more congruent with our abilities, passions, and age. And in all respects—whether in the home, the community, the market-place, or the church—we can see our work as a way in which we live under the kingdom reign of Christ and celebrate, through good times and difficult times, the reality that God is bringing His kingdom purposes into the world. The whole of our lives is lived in light of His kingdom, and this means that we no longer view parts of our lives as more sacred than others parts, but that all that we are—including our work—is lived under the king-dom reign of Jesus Christ.

THE KINGDOM AND A CHRISTIAN
UNDERSTANDING OF VOCATION

A recovery of Christ's understanding of God's work in the world (the kingdom) and of our work as creatures created in the image of God will help free the Christian community to appreciate the biblical character of *vocation*. Men and women are called to busi-ness, education, politics, the arts, and the sciences as well as to professional Christian ministry. The notion that professional ministry is a higher calling or superior vocation should be forever banished from our thinking. All vocations are kingdom voca-tions. All Christians are people of the kingdom *within* their voca-tions, as Christ uses all as His instruments of light, as His ambassadors of reconciliation.

Consequently, it is critical that we assist all Christians in dis-cerning their vocations, and then through the ministry of the church, equip them to fulfill their callings (Ephesians 4:12-15). The world has seldom seen the impact of a community of worshiping believers who gather together to encourage and equip one another for service within their God-given vocations. The Christian community can only be salt and light within society insofar as men and women are freed to respond to the full range of vocations for which God has enlisted His people.

As we seek to identify the essential components of a Christian spirituality, we do so with the full acknowledgment that different vocations require different spiritualities. All Christians—despite their vocations—seek a spirituality that is congruent with their calling. The basic elements of a Christian spirituality remain the same: the renewal of the mind, the encounter with God, service for God, accountability and structure, and finally, play and recreation. But we seek a form and structure to our spirituality that is congruent with the unique demands on our lives. For me, this means an extended prayer retreat each year. But a mother of four children can hardly plan on a retreat of this nature, and it may not be what she needs to help her be all that she is called to be. Those in business may require seminars and discussions about integrity in the marketplace as something integral to their work, whereas for someone called to education, the urgent need might be rather to foster a greater honesty of spirit and courage in his or her teaching. The components of a Christian spirituality remain the same, but the forms in which these components are found will vary from individual to individual—and a fundamental factor in shaping a spirituality will be the matter of vocation.

A conscious decision to make the whole of our lives spiritual, including our activity in the world, can show us how our role in the world can foster our union with Christ. How can our role as members of families and congregations, our occupation in the office or school, and our areas of responsibility and service be dimensions of our spirituality? There are at least five factors that determine whether our activity or vocation in the world is an integral part of our spirituality: it is in response to God's personal call; it is fulfilled with generosity and humility; through it we are prepared to meet God and hear His voice; we evaluate and measure its success on God's terms; and we have a present and a future orientation regarding time.

Recognizing God's Personal Call

The first factor is the recognition that our activity in the world is in response to God's personal call. We need to see that our task in the world—in its various dimensions—is in fulfillment of a divine call. It is a vocation, a calling. God longs to make all things well in the world, and He calls women and men to be coworkers with Him in this work.

James Fowler is very helpful on the subject of vocation in his book *Becoming Adult, Becoming Christian*.[3] Fowler seeks to understand the question of faith and vocation within the context of developmental psychology. He stresses that a Christian understanding of vocation establishes human activity in the purposes of God. We become His partners—coworkers with the Creator-Redeemer in His task of peacemaking. Vocation, then, is not our job, livelihood, or occupation. It may include this, but it is not limited to this. Vocation is not to be identified with profession or career. Our profession or career may be an expression of our divine calling—or vocation—but vocation is bigger than profession. Fowler writes,

> Vocation is the response a person makes with his or her total self to the address of God and to the calling to partnership. The shaping of vocation as total response of the self to the address of God involves the orchestration of our leisure, our relationships, our work, our private life, our public life, and of the resources we steward, so as to put it all at the disposal of God's purposes in the services of God and the neighbor.[4]

This view of vocation is liberating.[5] We are freed, for example, from competition with others. Each one has a unique calling or endowment that does not need to be established in competition. We no longer need fear that our vocation will be fulfilled by others; the opportunities are vast in number. We can rejoice and appreciate the gifts and abilities of others. Rather than envy other persons or be threatened by their abilities, we can freely appreciate their contribution to us and to the common good. We are not depreciated by the gifts and abilities of others.

Further, when we think in terms of vocation, we graciously accept who we are, and we serve out of that very identity. We do not wish we were someone else; we do not seek to be someone else. Rather, with courage and grace we embrace who we are and thus who we are called to be. In this I am impressed that in virtually every community there is a subtle hierarchy of vocations as we compare ourselves to one another and suggest how one is more important than the other. Such thinking is antithetical to the gospel. I was impressed when as a missionary in the Philippines I noticed that those who were establishing congregations were subtly treated as real missionaries, while those in theological education and development work were treated as second-class missionaries not doing the *real* work of a missionary. And now in academic life I also see the subtle suggestion that those involved as research scholars somehow have a superior calling to those who are in administration or those called to work as chaplains to the academic community. While we must affirm that there are some whose work is at the heart of the mission of the organization, we cannot thereby suggest that one calling is superior to another.

Then also, Fowler suggests that vocation is discerned in community. Consequently, not only do we then affirm that one's vocation must serve the common good, but also that vocation is not so much found as it is negotiated as one carves a place within the greater community. We shape our purposes in terms of the needs and purposes of the community. We live in mutual submission and mutual trust within that community. Fowler calls this community of faith "an ecology of vocations."[6]

Therefore, the first factor that determines whether our activity in the world is a component of our spirituality is whether we are acting in response to God's unique call upon our lives. (Appendix 3 suggests one question we might consider as we go about the task of discerning vocation.)[7]

Exercising Our Vocation with Generosity and Humility

A second factor that determines if our activity in the world is a dimension of our spiritual lives is the extent to which we are fulfilling our vocations with generosity and humility. We are God's servants, fulfilling our vocation in love for God and for our neighbor. An authentic vocation is literally lived for others. True service is richly rewarding and is a source of deep joy for us. But our activity in the world is counterproductive if it is governed by self-gratification and selfish ambition. Our motive is not "What is there in this for me?" but "Does this glorify God and help others?" We serve not with calculation, but with generosity. There is a joyful abandon in our desire to fulfill God's purposes and meet real needs. We eagerly help our children, make our home, serve our neighbors, and fulfill our daily occupations in response to God's generosity toward us. We therefore avoid calculated self-interest.

The call to humility is a call to serve God with sober minds, with full awareness of our gifts and our limitations. In discerning the call of God, we recognize that there is a corresponding endowment of ability, talent, and opportunity to fulfill this call. If God calls, then God equips. But God has not gifted us to do everything. Neither do we have supernatural mental skills and physical strength. We serve with generosity, but not with foolishness. There is a gentle tension between generosity and a recognition of one's limitations.

This understanding of our limitations is also liberating. We are freed from feeling the necessity of being all things to all people. We are not messiahs; we are not failures when we cannot fulfill all expectations. In vocation we experience our limits as well as our possibilities. Our responsibility is great but not unlimited. In this respect we are freed from overextending ourselves. We can freely have an appropriate level of participation in family, education, culture, economy, government, and church. We do not have to work to vindicate our worth. As a result, we are also freed from the tyranny of time. We are free to do what we are called to do . . . and for this there will always be plenty of time.

We previously explored in Mark 1 that after a day of generous service, Jesus got up and went to a solitary place to pray. His disciples came looking for Him, advising Him that there was great need for Him in Capernaum. But Jesus advised them—with great clarity of mind—that He was called to go on to other villages. Despite the clamor of Capernaum, Jesus turned from that city and went to others to fulfill His calling to preach. Surely, this would have disappointed the disciples. They would have been confused. Is this man a servant? Does He not care for the people of Capernaum? Jesus *did* care; He was a man of compassion, as we see so clearly in Mark 1 in His response to a leprous man. But Jesus had a calling to fulfill, and it was more important for Him to be a servant than to be known as a servant. In part, this is what it means to fulfill our vocations in humility. We cannot be all things to all people, despite our generosity. Those around us will not always understand this, but that is a small price to pay.

We cannot effectively fulfill our vocations or hear the voice of God in the course of our active and full days if we are busybodies. If we are physically, emotionally, or intellectually drained, we will not be fully in tune with our Lord. We can safely assume that God has a vocation or a calling for each of His people. But His yoke is easy—not in that there is little work to do. His yoke is easy in that it fits us just right. His yoke will challenge and stretch us and force us to depend on His grace. But frequently we take on additional weight, extra burdens that God did not intend for us. A good principle to remember is this: generous, willing people will always have more expectations to fulfill than they can possibly accomplish. Therefore, saying "no" and recognizing our limitations and our vocational focuses are part of true service.

Furthermore, the task to which we are called will include full identification with the Jesus who went to the cross and who in turn called His followers to take up the cross. Generosity means that it will *cost* us something. We choose to set aside ego for the well-being of the common good; we find that what matters to us most is not creature comforts, prestige, or recognition. Rather, we choose as much as we can to give heart and soul to the generous service of Jesus and His people.

But there are certain elements we cannot and need not sacrifice for the kingdom. We are not called to sacrifice our time in solitude with God, our marriages, or our children. Darrell Johnson, a colleague of mine at Regent College, has put it well: "God sacrificed His Son so that I would never need to sacrifice my son." This does not mean that we spend all our time in prayer or that we idolize the marriage or the family. Generous service will cost the spouse and the family also. But an authentic God-given vocation is wholly consistent with a healthy marriage and family life.

God *has* provided for the possibility of vocations (expressed through professions or church ministries) that involve long separations. His provision is celibacy (1 Corinthians 7). Some are called to singleness for the sake of the kingdom. But those who are married and have children are not free to sacrifice these life relationships for the sake of their vocations. To do so is to violate crucial dimensions of a Christian spirituality.

Meeting God in the World

A third factor that determines whether our activity in the world is a component of our spirituality is whether we are prepared to meet God and hear His voice in and through this activity. As parents, can we find God through our children? For business people, is God in the marketplace?

The apostle Peter met God in the world. When he was called of God to meet and respond to Cornelius, he suddenly discovered that the gospel was as much for the Gentile as for himself, a

Jew. He was converted! He found that the Spirit had preceded him in the world. Willing to meet God in the world and hear God's voice, Peter was turned around by what he discovered.

We cannot think of God as somehow being confined inside the walls of our churches or of our prayer closets. So frequently we tend to develop a "ghetto mentality" when we think of God's role in the world—that is, thinking that God is somehow *our* God and that He is Lord of the Christian community, while the Evil One is the lord of the world or of everything outside the confines of religious activity.

This is a faulty perception on two accounts. First, we cannot say that we are completely on God's side, because we know perfectly well that a battle wages continually in our minds. Spiritual warfare is principally a battle for the Christian mind—and the war is far from over. We are not perfect in motive. We still have much to learn; many areas of our thinking need conversion.

Second, this is a faulty perception of the world. As Peter came to discover, the Spirit of God was active in the world long before Peter appeared on the scene. The Scriptures confirm that God has left a witness of Himself in the conscience of every person. Every person, family, and culture can bear witness to God in some way. We have the potential of learning from all the people we meet—whether believers or not. God can speak to us in many ways if we are prepared to see and listen.

I remember distinctly an experience I had as a young university student in Regina, Canada. I was a volunteer responsible for the book table sponsored and run by a group of Christians meeting on campus. For a few hours each week I would be there meeting passersby, selling books or just tending the book table. The hallway in which our table was set up included several other groups selling books, including Marxists, Marxist-Leninists, Hari Krishnas, and anarchists (who, it seemed to me, always maintained the neatest book table). One day, a student I had not seen before came by and asked me for a book on economic injustice and the problem of world poverty.

"I have none," I said. Then he asked me where he could get books on the subject, and it struck me that across the hall was a table full of books addressing the very theme, but from a Marxist perspective. I was stunned, and I realized that my circle of faith and thinking had not addressed this important problem adequately. Ironically, it was through the Marxists that I first realized that there was something very wrong with the world economic order. Eventually, I came to find that God was very concerned about this problem and that there is indeed a fine body of literature from a Christian perspective that addresses this concern. But it was the Marxists whom God used to point it out to me, at least initially.

Part of meeting God in the world includes learning and discovery, discerning His presence ahead of us, and hearing His voice even through those who do not affirm His lordship. But to see and hear God in the world also means responding with openness to suffering, difficulty, and failure.

We are often of the mind that our goal in life is happiness. Many choose to follow the Christian faith because they want an easy, comfortable, problem-free life, and they believe that in Jesus they will find this. But God's purposes are bigger. He desires that we become righteous. Christ's objective as the ascended Lord of the church is to present each of us spotless before the Father, that through the Word we would be made whole (Ephesians 5:25-27). Thus, Christ tests our faith, allows us to be tempted, and permits the Evil One to stretch us to the edge of our limits (but no more), which is not necessarily happiness. Through stress and distress, God is near; we find our Lord and hear His voice in both the long easy stretches as well as along more difficult roads.

If we are not prepared to see and know God in the world, we will not be freed to grow in holiness. But if we regard every personal encounter, every obstacle in our path, and every difficulty as further means by which we can hear God's voice and experience His grace, then, the largest part of our waking hours (our vocation in the world) will foster spiritual vitality.

Success and Christian Vocation

If God calls and equips us to fulfill a calling, then can we be confident we will know success? No, not necessarily. Even if God did guarantee our success, what is success from God's perspective? These are crucial questions as we reflect on a Christian understanding of work and vocation. Our service — our activity in the world — cannot be a component of our spirituality unless we evaluate and measure success on God's terms rather than cultural ones. This is a fourth factor that determines the extent to which our task in the world is a component of a Christian spirituality.

To start with, we need to remember that God delights in working through human notions of failure, weakness, and vulnerability. We have no guarantee of visible, outward success. God has called us to be faithful in fulfilling the task He has given to each of us, and often the most significant work that He will accomplish will be through what is perceived in the world as failure. But it seems fair to say that if God calls and equips us for a task, He usually expects to fulfill His purposes through us. As we accomplish that task, hopefully we are effective in the responsibilities He has given to us. But we still need to rethink our notions of success. We can identify four characteristics of a biblical understanding of success.

First, success in the kingdom of God is a relative matter. We tend to evaluate all people on an equal basis and by a standard measurement. In school, some students receive good grades and some poor grades. In some cases this reflects the student's discipline and commitment, but it also is evidence of intelligence and ability. The grading system is not wrong in itself, but it does not necessarily reflect kingdom values. In God's kingdom some have received five talents, a few ten, and others only one talent. And the freedom we have is that we are evaluated accordingly.

This could be understood more broadly. We are responsible — and are judged successful by God — to the extent that we have been faithful stewards of the abilities, gifts, resources, and opportunities we have. We are evaluated individually; and in the end only God can make a fair statement of our success or failure. Only God can see the whole picture.

Second, in the kingdom of God there is no success in the Christian community at the expense of others. We are all winners or all losers. Competition in terms of numbers, influence, and status are simply incompatible with kingdom values. God's calling and God's vision are unique to individuals and organizations, but they are also complementary to other vocations and visions.

Third, in the kingdom, success is not the only—or even the highest—ideal. We are not committed to success at any expense. A commitment to an ideal or vision of success can blind us to other priorities and other kinds of work God is doing. God can and often does some of His most remarkable work through our failures. When we are weak, He has the means by which to display His strength and glory. But even when we do have valid ideals, our success will be a false one if in the pursuit of our goals we compromise ourselves or our vocations. Success is not the highest value in the kingdom.

Finally, for God, bigger is not necessarily better. In 1985 there was a massive multi-city, global broadcast of a conference for young people. Manila was one of the sites for this simultaneous program. I will never forget the sense of awe that struck people at the thought of such a massive production. The global conference was a success, but who knows whether God considered it a critical kingdom event.

We tend to be impressed by grand-scale technological wizardry. But this is not the case with God. God values holiness, faith, love, and good works. He sees significance and eternal worth in what may be very small in our eyes. For example, Jesus saw meaning in the two coins of the widow, in contrast to the more impressive giving of others. In the kingdom, the widow's two small coins meant far more. We tend to be impressed by big churches, big programs, and confident personalities who have education, great speaking or musical abilities, and wealth. But God sees things differently, and if we are to find success and foster union with Christ through our activity in the world, we need to be aligned with His perspective.

A Kingdom View of Time

Finally, another evidence that our spirituality is authentic — truly a kingdom spirituality — is a radically different perception of time. Generally speaking, there are two classic heresies with respect to an understanding of time. Some view all meaningful time as occurring in the future. They live for the future. The present is merely a stepping-stone for the future, and all their energies are devoted to accomplishing something yet ahead of them. Their vision arises out of a conviction that great things can be accomplished for God, and they view time as wasted when it is not used in practical ways that meet goals and objectives. The error here is that this perspective of time denies that the kingdom has come. Regardless of how wonderful plans and goals may be, the kingdom is present. Jesus has come; the Incarnation led to the death and resurrection of the Christ! We can relax — Christ is Lord! Consequently, our work or activity in this world is not merely a means to an end. It glorifies God in itself. It can be a joyful foretaste of the consummated kingdom. We distort time when we are driven to work purely in order to have something in the future.

But then there are those for whom the future can wait. They love life and probably feel that the future will be what it will be. They will live tomorrow tomorrow. They appreciate the seasons of life, the daily routine of work and friends and food. They feel at peace with God and with creation. They are convinced that there is time enough for everything. But this too is a heresy, a partial truth. The kingdom is not yet consummated. The sin lurking within our own minds and the horrendous injustices that characterize our societies are surely a daily and sufficient reminder that we must be about the Master's business.

The solution to these two heresies is found in a renewed appreciation of the Incarnation and the kingdom. In the

Incarnation we have the union of time and eternity in the person of Christ Jesus. In the Incarnation we have the union of the mystical and earthly. In Christ we have the fulfillment of the kingdom.

Although the kingdom will be consummated in Christ, we stand now in a tension between fulfillment and consummation. We must therefore have both a present and a future orientation. We can live in peace and rest in the confidence that the kingdom has come; we also need to live with a holy dissatisfaction with the circumstances around us and to strive in the grace of God to be agents of kingdom redemption.

Time is so frequently viewed as a nonrenewable resource. But think about this for a moment. Regardless of how you respond to the next hour in your life, you will have just as many hours left in your day. Time is a gift from God, an opportunity to be responded to. It is more helpful to think of time as something that is filled rather than as something that is used. Then, instead of bemoaning the passing of time, we can delight in each new moment, each new day, each new season. We can graciously accept time and the passing of years.

In this perspective, then, a spirituality is merely a structure or a routine for responding joyfully and effectively to the gift of time. We need to be preserved from the tendency to rush passionately through time and thereby miss the voice of God and the signs of the kingdom. But we need equally to be preserved from the life that fails to fulfill its potential. We are called both to abide in Christ *and* to serve Christ. Joy and effectiveness within our vocations come from a gentle and steady rhythm of abiding in the Lord, on the one hand, and serving the Lord, on the other.

CHAPTER

◆ ◆ ◆ ◆ 5

SPIRITUAL AUTHORITY AND ACCOUNTABILITY

We live in a spiritual age that elevates the value of spontaneity and resists thinking that structure, order, obedience, accountability, and routine might be life-giving. These are the four-letter words of a whole generation. But the wisdom of our spiritual heritage suggests just the opposite: there is freedom in obedience, structure, and order.

Further, when we live under the reign of Christ, we live very specifically under the *authority* of Christ. Who we are and what we do come in response to this authority. And the Christian tradition would call us to appreciate that we do not live under Christ's authority until and unless we learn to live intentionally under the authority of others. These "others" are representatives of Christ to us.

THE NEED FOR ACCOUNTABILITY

St. Ignatius Loyola spoke of a willingness to call what is black white and what is white black if it were so directed or decreed by the Catholic Church. Protestants usually respond to this with horror and indignation. For a Protestant, black would only be white and white black if there were chapter and verse in Holy Writ that indicated as much. But though Protestants and many contemporary Catholics recoil from the hierarchicalism of Ignatius and his apparent unthinking subservience, a closer look reveals that he was affirming a cardinal principle of the spiritual life—submission to authority. We may not appreciate the way this principle was expressed, but spiritual submission is an essential component of a Christian spirituality. The vow of obedience that characterized the spiritual life of Ignatius was unique, but the principle of accountability is a universal one for the Christian community.

This is perhaps *the* component of Christian spirituality that is most lacking among contemporary Protestants. The Reformation affirmed the right of the individual to hear the voice of God, to worship God through Christ without the mediation of a priest, and to understand the Scriptures in one's own language. But this individualism, while affirming valid biblical truths, had the unfortunate tendency to undercut other equally valid truths—specifically, the principle of spiritual authority and accountability. Christians somehow came up with the idea that they are autonomous and stand alone before God with no direct accountability to the church or the authority of church leadership. But the weight of the scriptural evidence strongly supports the principle of authority and accountability. The lack of this component represents a spiritually dangerous state of affairs.

Many Christians live as spiritual hermits. Our interior lives are secret worlds known only to ourselves. In some cases the dark corners of our lives are unknown to us because we have failed to live up to them and face them honestly and courageously. In part we are afraid of these dark shadows of our souls. As Protestants, we tend to live in spiritual isolation, confessing to no one, acknowledging little of what happens in our inner worlds, and experiencing little deep spiritual friendship. We lack structures of spiritual accountability. And many of us resist them. Whether it comes to the inner life or the patterns of our work, words like submission, obedience, and accountability make us cringe. We are lone rangers—whether in work or in prayer—and we resist anyone who might suggest that our lives are not our own and that anyone else can tell us how we should live. While we certainly must affirm the critical need for personal responsibility and while we must at the same time resist the abuse of power and authority, the principle of spiritual submission and obedience needs to be placed before us.

Spiritual obedience is one of the marks of the church. In Scripture we are called to confess our sins to one another and to live in mutual submission, humbling ourselves before each other within the Christian community. Even the apostles were accountable to one another, as evidenced by the Jerusalem Council. The apostle Paul speaks of the need for mutual submission, of obedience to those assigned to spiritual leadership, whether they be pastors, elders, or bishops. Although the move away from this dimension of the spiritual life might be traced by some to the Protestant Reformation, the Reformers themselves — and John Wesley after them — cannot be faulted for failing to call for accountability. Each of them acknowledged the priesthood of all believers, but also stressed the principle of spiritual authority within the church. Wesley is well known for the intense small-group meetings that characterized the Methodist movement. There were no Wesleyan individualists. To be part of this movement of spiritual renewal meant that one was actively involved either as a member of a "band" or in what was called a "class," which was a group that met regularly for mutual accountability and ministry.

Wesley believed that our need for accountability needed to find tangible and concrete expression if our spiritual lives are to have stability and continual growth. We are not spiritual monads; authentic Christianity cannot be lived in isolation as an interior hermit.

David Augsburger notes the importance of this for all Christians, but places particular stress on those in leadership. He warns that public ministry is in constant danger of destroying the leader if appropriate channels of accountability are not in place. He insists that mutual accountability and interdependence are essential to overcome the individualism of Western Christianity.

Augsburger suggests that our egalitarian society, having abandoned vertical models of authority, has failed to replace these with models of mutual accountability and community.[1]

We tend to think of authority figures as people who make our lives unpleasant or as people who put limits on our joy and freedom. But in fact, living under identifiable authority grants us both perspective and freedom. I enjoy playing squash, a racket sport. I also enjoy *thinking* about the game. In squash, in contrast to tennis, the player who wins is usually the one who is able to control the center of the court. Both players play on the same side of the "net," so to speak, using all four sides of a small room. And we win our points by forcing the other player to play first one side and then the other. When I was receiving instruction, the trainer kept insisting that after every shot I needed to return quickly and as effortlessly as possible to the center of the court. From there I could with two strides return just about any shot from my opponent. When I lost a point, it was usually because I was caught off-center.

In the same way, authority in our lives is like a central point of reference, something we can come back to again and again to give us perspective and to prepare us for just about anything that comes our way. Without structures of authority, we are less likely to keep our bearings and be prepared for what comes up in our lives. The squash player who controls the center actually has more freedom to respond, not less, because of the restraints that come with returning to the center after every stroke.

Further, our spiritual heritage also affirms that we need spiritual authority and accountability as a means to check our own misguided motives and keep us humble. There is no true humility that does not, in some form, find expression in relationship with others.

POTENTIAL FORMS OF ACCOUNTABILITY

What I would hope is that as we think through what it means to be *on the way*, we would acknowledge the dangers of spiritual isolation. But then we need to also think positively about this dimension of the spiritual life and to activate potential structures for living in submission to others. The authority of Christ's lordship over our lives can and will be expressed through a variety of forms and ministries: submission to the preached Word, Sacrament, and church authority; small-group interaction; spiritual friendship or direction; intergenerational relationships; and spiritual reading.

The Formal Ministry and Authority of the Church

First, it is essential that we live in submission to the preached Word and the administered Sacrament. The Christian cannot know spiritual vitality unless he or she knows the power of spiritual preaching and the nourishment of the spiritual food of the Lord's Table. Yet these only have meaning if the believer lives in submission to the one that God has placed in the ministry as preacher and pastor. We need to recognize during each worship event that Christ is speaking to us and feeding us—in the Word and Sacrament—through a *person,* a fellow human being. Christ can only minister to us if we worship Him in submission to His appointed servants.

This also pertains to our lives as members of the church. Authentic Christian life includes full congregational life. We are part of a Christian community, and community is impossible without submission. Each community has elders or comparable individuals who are the recognized spiritual leaders of the assembly. They have real authority. But then we also appreciate that within congregational life we are called to live in mutual submission to one another. No one stands alone, not even the pastor or preacher. All are called to live in community. In many forms of church government, this means that we acknowledge the authority represented by the vote of the majority. Submission to constituted authority means that we accept with grace the formal decisions that are made, quite apart from whether we agree with or have voted with the majority.

This form of spiritual accountability also finds expression within the organizations where we work. I think a case could be made that *all* of us are called to spiritual submission and account-ability in the workplace, regardless of whether or not those to whom we report are Christians. But as I work within a theological school, it is a vital part of my spirituality to live with a conscious recognition that I am called to spiritual submission within clearly defined lines of accountability. As vice president and dean, I report to a president, and together we live in intentional accountability to the board of the school. Further, I view my task as one that includes accountability to the faculty. Even though there is certainly a sense in which they report to me in their work, I nevertheless view my work as one in which I am intentionally responsible to them. And my point in all of this is that this is not merely a professional understanding; it is as *spiritual* an act as anything I do, as vital a part of my spiritual walk as Bible study, prayer, and worship.

Small Groups

Though the patterns of accountability and submission are very important in the church and in the workplace, we are well advised to also pursue patterns of accountability that are more intentional and focused. Our Christian heritage commends two good alternatives to us in this regard. Both are models that can effectively break down the barrier of isolation that characterizes the inner lives of so many Christian believers. One model is the small group; the other is the spiritual director or friend.

Many Christians find it valuable to be part of a small group that serves as a close community of peers. These groups can take a variety of forms, but ideally a group should meet regularly every week or two for reflection on the Scriptures, sharing of personal concerns (including areas of failure), encouragement and counsel between the participants, and prayer. Many times, leaders within congregational life are involved in small-group ministries, but usually in a pastoral or study-leader capacity. The genius of these kinds of groups is that the leader is only a facilitator or coordinator of the time together. The group comprises a gathering of peers who exercise mutual accountability and mutual ministry.

Spiritual Friendship and Direction

Relationships within a small group can be invaluable. But there is another form of accountability that needs to be profiled. Christians of many diverse backgrounds and traditions are rediscovering the vital place of a spiritual friend and director, something that Roman Catholics in religious orders have known for centuries. A spiritual friend or director (I will use these terms interchangeably) is that individual with whom we openly discuss and reflect on the inner pilgrimage of our lives. He or she is that individual in whose presence the inner recesses of our minds and hearts are no longer so secret. In a formal relationship, the heart of spiritual direction is the act of guiding the prayer life of a fellow pilgrim; informally, a spiritual friend is a fellow pilgrim we trust for guidance, encouragement, and counsel, and with whom we feel sufficiently accepted so that we are free to confess our sins.

Alan Jones cites two reasons why it is profitable for a Christian to have a spiritual director.[2] I will add a third. (These three reasons apply also to the value of a small group.) First, we need a spiritual director because of our capacity for self-deception. Those who acknowledge a need for spiritual direction and friendship are people who have no illusions about their own spiritual maturity and strength. This recognition arises out of a genuine humility. The heart is deceptively wicked. Our motives are far from pure, however much we might wish they were sanctified. We need a friend—a director—who can ask us the questions we may well be avoiding.

The friends who love us most do so unreservedly, but also with discrimination. They do not love blindly or foolishly. The book of Proverbs includes many descriptions of genuine friendship. We note in Proverbs 27:6 that a true friend is characterized by candor. A false friend flatters, but "well meant are the wounds a friend inflicts" (note also Proverbs 28:23). In other words, spiritual friendship includes a willingness to confront and to challenge motives, actions, and priorities. We enter willingly into this kind of a relationship because of our capacity for self-deception. We need the honesty of a true friend. We need to know—without doubt—that there is someone who is candid with us.

Second, a spiritual director is also of great value because of our constant need for hope. Our tasks in the world are filled with obstacles and difficulties. Each of us has a vocation, but we seem to encounter failure and frustration at every turn. We lose hope; our courage wanes. We all need an encourager—someone to restore our hope. But encouragement consists of empty words when it is not accompanied by love. Our hope is restored when we are reassured and reminded of God's grace and work while confident of love and acceptance. We must not underestimate the transforming power of divine love working through our director. We all need this love, expressed through reassuring words—a love that restores our hope, renews our vision, and reestablishes our confidence in God. And we need it constantly, again and again.

Third, we need a spiritual friend to serve as a co-discerner when we are making important decisions in our lives. This includes questioning motives with candor and honesty. It includes giving encouragement so that by divine grace we can fulfill God's call for us. But more specifically, we need someone to help us listen to God's voice when we come to a fork in the road. A spiritual director can assist by helping us discern our feelings and motives during prayer; a friend can hear us and help weigh pros and cons of the choices we face. By direction, I do not mean that they will be the Spirit to us nor that they tell us what to do. No. Spiritual friends do not replace the guidance of the Holy Spirit. Rather, they can serve as co-discerners. They help us see and hear the voice of the Lord clearly and encourage us to respond wholeheartedly.

In his book *Come Down Zacchaeus*, Thomas Green has suggested that we should look for four qualities in choosing a spiritual director.[3] First, he should be someone with whom we are comfortable; second, she should be someone who understands what we are seeking in our prayer and spirituality; third, he should be able to respond objectively in interpreting our personal experience in prayer; and fourth, she should ideally be someone whom we recognize as further ahead of us in the spiritual pilgrimage. Good directors are hard to find, and some of us may not be able to find an older, wiser person. However, we can always find someone, a peer perhaps, with whom we can have meaningful spiritual conversation.

The spiritual director or friend is an important person in our circle of accountability. This person probably plays a critical role in our lives. But a full and complete humanity is expressed and fulfilled in a wide range of relationships. We are not hermits, however quiet or retiring our personalities may be. Authentic spirituality is lived in community. Some of the most outgoing people are lonely on the inside; they sometimes have few intimate and intentional personal relationships.

I would suggest that each adult should have about twenty meaningful relationships. We each need at least twenty individuals who play a significant role in our lives: in our families, in our workplace, in our church, and among neighbors and friends. These are mutual and reciprocal relationships consisting of friends (probably no more than three or four) and acquaintances who know us well. This network of relationships is essential for a healthy emotional, psychological, and spiritual life. And each relationship in some form or another represents but another way in which Christ is present to us and by which we are accountable to Christ.

Intergenerational Relationships

Any discussion of an intentional relationship within the life of the Christian believer should also profile what is clearly highlighted within Holy Scripture. When Paul writes to Timothy and Titus, he outlines a whole range of relationships that he assumes will bring strength to the community as a whole and will assure that individuals mature in faith, hope, and love. For example, he speaks of the need for older women to teach younger women (Titus 2:3-4) and thus follows his own advice by providing spiritual guidance for a younger man. This speaks to a vital relationship for each Christian: the need for blessing, encouragement, and wisdom from older men to younger men, from older women to younger women.

While there may be an element of accountability to such a relationship, I urge younger people to seek out those who are older for a simple reason: they need them. One generation needs the blessing of the generation that preceded it; young people need the blessing of those who are older. They need their counsel, the wisdom of years lived and life experienced. They need their friendship. I cannot imagine where I would be in life and work were it not for the older men along the way who were present to me and gave generously of their time. What I suggest is simply this: for every chapter of your life, find an older person, perhaps in your place of study or work, perhaps in the congregation with which you gather for worship, or perhaps in the community where you live. For each transition of life and each new chapter in your life, find someone who is older and buy them lunch, get together over coffee, or make it a pattern to take a walk with him or her every so often.

Spiritual Reading

There is yet another means by which we can live intentionally under spiritual authority. Spiritual accountability can be exercised through spiritual reading—the careful, meditative reading of the devotional or spiritual classics. This is reading designed to increase not merely knowledge about God, but also personal, intimate knowledge of God. It is valuable to read the spiritual classics as literature, reflecting on the piety of another age in the history of the church. But spiritual reading is different, for it arises out of a conviction that within the universal church God has gifted some individuals to express remarkably, for all ages, the nature of the spiritual life and what A. W. Tozer calls, "the deep things of God." We view these authors not as ancient historical figures but as pastors and teachers to Christians even today. Martin Luther still serves as a pastor to the twenty-first century through his writings; Bernard of Clairvaux still serves as a director of the spiritual life through his *On the Love of God*.

It needs to be stressed, though, that spiritual reading of this kind can never be viewed as a substitute for or replacement for accountability to a person who is alive and present to us and genuinely able to call us to accountability. But when these other forms of genuine accountability are in place, spiritual reading is unquestionably a vital way by which we root our lives in the historic spiritual traditions of the church.

Spiritual reading is done with an open heart, a submissive mind, and a willingness to hear God's voice and follow Him. It is different from academic reading, which fosters objectivity, critical analysis, and detachment. But the problem with this kind of reading is that it suggests that we stand over the text as critics of the writer. And while academic reading has its place, spiritual reading sustains another critical and essential value in our lives: the capacity to be mastered by the text, for we are no longer detached but genuinely placing ourselves in accountability to the text. We read from an inner posture of submission to the pastors and teachers of the greater Christian community, opening our lives to their penetrating words. (See Appendix 4 for a list of recommended devotional classics and a suggested approach to reading them.) I should, though, also add that a genuine academic education includes learning how to read both ways: we read and learn critical analysis, and also we read and learn how to open heart and mind to what we read.

In all of these suggestions, though, nothing of genuine spiritual accountability will happen unless we are intentional. Whether we follow these actual suggestions or not, it is up to us to design structures of spiritual authority and accountability that will provide us with counsel, encouragement, and direction. Some may wish they could find a good director; admittedly, trained spiritual direction is rare and sometimes hard to find. But we can approach each chapter of our lives with a simple assumption: the grace of God will be available to us; we simply need to nurture the relationships that God *does* give us rather than bemoan what seems to us to be missing.

THE DANGER OF AUTHORITARIANISM AND SPIRITUAL DEPENDENCE

There is an attendant danger to certain forms of spiritual direction that we must be aware of: authoritarianism and spiritual dependence. In *Exploring Spiritual Direction,* Alan Jones notes that spiritual direction lends itself to abuse. People long for authority figures; cults are built around strong religious, authoritarian models. Because spiritual direction is based on submission and obedience, exploitation is so very possible and can be a constant temptation. People seek guidance; they are sheep seeking a shepherd. And often there will be men and women who are quite prepared to exploit the needs and vulnerability of people seeking help. Often the very people seeking guidance and counsel are not discriminating in their search for direction and spiritual friendship. We need to restore the place of spiritual direction in the life of the church; but just as surely, as Jones insists, there are pitfalls to avoid.[4]

Some teachers and writers today have so emphasized authority and accountability that they forget the importance of individual responsibility. They regard human authority—whether parents, employers, pastors, or government leaders—as deserving complete and unquestioned obedience. They distort an otherwise essential and good component of the Christian life. All human authority is conditional, not absolute. Ultimate authority belongs only to God. Even parents need to recognize that authentic parenting basically consists of leading a child to mature responsibility for his or her own life under the authority of God. Government officials who undermine justice and pastors who fail to preach the Word or administer the Lord's Supper can surely be questioned by the discerning Christian. Blind submission is irresponsible.

Those in positions of spiritual authority—whether parents, pastors, church elders, or spiritual directors—must appreciate that their role is to serve Christ. A preacher should be able to say confidently to his congregation, "If you don't find it in the Scriptures, don't take it from me." True preaching leads people to the Word, not to the preacher. Elders within a congregation are called by God not to lord it over their flock but to be examples. The very same text that calls us to acknowledge the authority of elders (1 Peter 5:5) also insists that elders must not lord it over those whom they serve (5:3). Spiritual directors should never demand blind followers; they should only serve as catalysts to spiritual maturity and depth. They are midwives of the spiritual life.

Therefore, true spiritual direction can eventually lead to spiritual friendship between director and directee, because what is sought is interdependence, not dependence. False spiritual authority encourages dependence; true spiritual authority fosters maturity in people, enabling them to become responsible, contributing members of a body of believers. The same principle applies to the work of counseling: the objective is not creating dependence but providing individuals with the mental, emotional, and spiritual tools to be mature members of a community.

This is often difficult for Christians to handle. Some prefer to remain in a position of dependence. As a father, I sometimes needed to push my two sons a little further than they wanted to go; otherwise they would not mature. They needed to move from dependence on their earthly parents to interdependence as fellow adults and, of course, to dependence on their heavenly Father.

In the group prayer retreats I lead, the prayer times are designed to be personal encounters with Christ. Often, real and profound needs of the retreatants are brought to the surface; participants are anxious for help as they discern the Word of the

Lord. Although I am there to help, I have a simple rule: I will only meet with the retreatants for a few minutes at a time. It may seem much too short to the needy retreatant, but the time is long enough. After the retreat, there will be time to talk, but during the retreat, the goal is that the participants spend time with Christ. Figuratively speaking, I seek to throw them back in Christ's arms where they ultimately belong and where they will need to go on their own if they are to mature in their faith. We all need spiritual direction and friendship. But this must ultimately lead to a deeper spiritual maturity and a closer relationship with Christ Himself.

ROUTINE AND RHYTHM

What I am seeking to stress is that while spiritual accountability and authority are vital elements in the Christian life, nothing takes the place of personal responsibility for one's own life before God. And one of the ways in which we assume this responsibility is evident in the pattern of discipline that marks our daily and weekly routines.

Our lives are living confessions of the peace of God when they are characterized by order. An orderly life does not preclude freedom and spontaneity. It merely affirms that there is no freedom without form; there is no spontaneity without structure. Part of the beauty of the monastic tradition is the simplicity and consistency of the routine and rhythms of daily life. It follows that we would appreciate that as we long for freedom we should strive for order—routine and rhythm in our own experience.

First, then, we need a rhythm of solitude and community. A full Christian experience includes solitude—for study, prayer, and even elements of play—complemented by community—again for study, prayer, service, and play. There is a balance between the individual and personal dimensions of our spirituality and the dimensions we live as part of a community of like-minded believers. Each of the five essential components of an authentic spirituality—study, prayer, vocation, accountability, and recreation—should have an individual as well as a corporate expression. We study alone; we study in community. We know the prayer of solitude; we participate in the public worship of the people of God. We have learned to work alone in the service of God; we also have developed the ability to work with others. We have individual lines of accountability (a spiritual director or friend); we are also potentially a part of a small group of peers for encouragement and accountability. And, we have a hobby and the freedom to spend time alone; we have learned the joy of friendships and recreation with others. The spiritual life includes both dimensions—the individual and the community.

Second, we need routine in our daily lives. This does not imply adherence to strict legalistic rules. But we are creatures of habit, and we function best in routine. The five components—study, prayer, vocation, accountability, and recreation—do not need to be part of each day, and we will certainly not have equal amounts of each component. But the freedom of routine is still possible. For example, our week could be a routine of six and one, of active fulfillment of our responsibilities in the world, complemented by a day of recreation. Our day may include prayer, work, and recreation, which we live out in a consistent and orderly fashion. And the evident order of our lives assures that each of the essential components of a Christian spirituality is truly integrated into our experience.

Order—routine and rhythm—is by itself a discipline that confers a balance among the various components of the Christian life and between the individual and communal aspects of our spirituality.

RECREATION

A true spirituality encompasses the whole of our lives as they are lived under God. As we seek to live under and in terms of the reign of Christ, we must necessarily speak of a spirituality that includes both prayer and work. But just as surely, we need to speak of the place of recreation. Leisure in various forms is part of every whole and balanced life. It too, of necessity, must be a component of our spirituality. We need to see leisure and recreation as under the grace of God and therefore as contributing an essential element to our spirituality. Indeed, recreation could be viewed as an actual discipline or practice of the spiritual life. But recreation is a dynamic element of our spiritual lives only when we see it as part of what it means to live in the light of the reign of Christ and the coming of His kingdom.

SABBATH RESTS

The theological basis for play or recreation is found in the principle of the Sabbath rest. God created the earth in six days, and on the seventh He rested. Then God ordained that the Hebrew week was to be a rhythm of six and one, a work week followed by a day in which work was prohibited.

For many people, the principle of Sabbath rest has come to mean a day of religious activities—the more religion the better. There are many from my generation who came to dislike Sundays because we were taught it was a day in which we were to do religious things—notably, going to public services. Sunday was not to be a day of recreation, but a day of "rest."

Christians are realizing more and more what Jesus meant when He said that the Sabbath was made for people and not people for the Sabbath. The Sabbath is a day God reserves for us—for the best part of life, for both the enjoyment of the Lord in worship and also the enjoyment of His creation through recreation. Certainly we need to gather with God's people for worship and ministry. But in the affirmation of the Sabbath we also highlight that we require rest, renewal, and recreation. The Sabbath is a day to cease from our labors as we enjoy the fruit of God's work and ours—delighting in our families, our friends, our homes and neighborhoods, as well as delighting in God.

While I was in my growing-up years, my community used to think that the Sabbath was the Lord's Day, which in turn meant it was a day of religious activities; in this day it seems we have a very different problem. The hectic pace of life has left more and more people with a propensity toward continual work. While they may fit in religious activities here and there, what marks their lives more than anything is the pattern of business, deadlines, and overwork that leaves them in what seems to be a perpetual state of exhaustion. Their lives are *filled* with their work and with the many demands on their time. Our businesses and commercial establishments now run not only seven days a week, but in some places even twenty-four hours a day over those seven days! We cannot get away from work, including the work of buying and selling.

Observance of Sabbath rest is grounded in the conviction that there is more to life than our work. God has given us work to do to glorify Him and sustain our lives and those of our dependents. But life is not all work. In withdrawing consistently and regularly from our work we declare that we are more than our work and that our identity and provision lies finally in God and not in the fruit of our hands.

LIVING WITH HOPE

Understanding the theological foundation for recreation begins, perhaps, with considering the place of Sabbath, but it also includes an examination of the nature of the kingdom and the place of hope in our lives. Through leisure and recreation we proclaim with our actions that we are a people of *hope*. There is no doubt that the world is broken; every day the newspaper reminds us of the depth of the human predicament. If we play, if we take time for friends, hobbies, sports, and the arts, it is *not* because we are blind to the severity of the human need. Rather, our play or recreation is rooted in our hope—our conviction that there is more to reality than meets the eye. We believe that Christ is on the throne of the universe and that because of a victory already accomplished over evil, Christ will make all things well in His time. Our times of rest and recreation are a profound proclamation of this hope.

This hope is based on a particular understanding of the kingdom of God, and this understanding in turn has dramatic implications for our lives. We live in truth when we walk in the reality that the kingdom has come but that it will as yet come in all its fullness. Theologians speak, then, of the kingdom as *already* but *not yet*. This reality shapes the way we *think*—we believe something about the kingdom. But it also necessarily is translated into the way we *live*. Recreation is a declaration that we believe the kingdom has already come. While we are not naïve to believe or suggest that it has come in all its completeness, we can nevertheless act in concrete, tangible ways that demonstrate this confidence. We know the kingdom *has* come; and we know it *will* come. And further, we know that its coming will not depend on our actions. Therefore, we can *play*; recreation is an extraordinary demonstration of this hope.

I served as a pastor for several years for a small congregation in central Ontario. One evening, we were holding a church board meeting while a storm was raging outdoors. The longer we deliberated, the more it snowed. And unfortunately, we discussed and debated long into the evening. I lived twenty miles out of the city and I was eager to get home to my family. When the meeting finally ended, I was soon in my car and on my way home. In my hurry I chose to take an alternate, shorter route. With the heavy snowfall, I should have kept to the main highway. Yet I thought if I could just keep the car moving, I would not get caught up in the snowdrifts.

Well, the further I got down that back road, the higher the drifts seemed to be. Just when I was thinking that I might make it through, I came on a very high snowdrift and plowed in before I had a chance to stop. There I was, miles from help, sitting in a car that was stalled, on a cold, stormy night.

Well, I was young and hearty, so I jumped out with the shovel in hand that I had for just such occasions. I attacked the snow with the thought that it would be but a few minutes before I was on my way. But the drift was much too large, and after fifteen minutes I knew that I had no hope of digging my way out. I began to look up and down the road, hoping that some heavenly tow truck would appear. But, naturally, no one was on that road in that kind of weather!

So I had no choice but to close up the car and head off on foot. To my surprise, over the very next hill I saw a light and soon I came upon a farmhouse. I knocked at the door, asked to use the phone, called my friend, and received immediate assurance that he would be there in about twenty minutes.

I returned to the car, sat on the hood, and took in the evening. It was the most beautiful winter evening I have ever experienced. The storm was over. The moon was high by then. In the quiet I saw motion to one side and turned in time to see a rabbit scurry away. A quiet hush ruled the valley, and though I was alone, I was at peace.

Before I had left for the farmhouse, I was desperately hoping that help would come along that road. But after the phone call, I had hope. I *knew* that my friend was coming. And that hope gave me a powerful serenity that enabled me to see the beauty of a winter night and enjoy the quiet that comes after a storm.

As Christians, this is what we mean by hope—a posture of confidence regarding the future that gives us peace in the present. And each time we stop our work and enjoy our world and our friends, we are reminded of that hope. Our play, then, gives perspective to the whole of our lives. It is a vital element of a spirituality that is grounded in the reality of the kingdom.

OUR NEED FOR REST

There is yet another reason for recreation. We need rest. As people who love Christ and long to serve Him wholeheartedly, we easily become overextended in our daily responsibilities. Many work seven days a week on the pretext that their vocation, their specific role or responsibility, demands relentless attention. The truth is that no one is indispensable. In failing to rest and withdraw from our work or ministry, we are essentially saying that we are somehow irreplaceable. The consequence is often a life that loses its compassionate edge and eventually its personal dimension. We become exhausted or burned out fulfilling a God-given vocation.

We need not be impressed by those who say they work seven days a week. It would be more appropriate for us to express our concern or perhaps a word of caution. We all need to withdraw periodically to rest and enjoy the fruit of God's work. In so doing, we live in joyful anticipation of our ultimate Sabbath rest, which will come with the consummation of Christ's kingdom.

Actually, the principle of Sabbath rest involves much more than merely one day a week. It refers to that whole dimension of our lives where we live in simple, childlike joy under God's mercy as His redeemed people. We rest from our vocations at some point every day, not just one day a week; we delight in God's created order and His gifts to us—every day, not just one day in seven.

Many Christians need to learn to play. They have consciences that frequently leave them guilty, hesitant, and inhibited, because they feel play is a questionable activity. They have grown up with a work ethic that assumes all redeemed time is devoted to work. For too long we have simply neglected play as a fundamental dimension of a full Christian life.

SABBATH AS RECREATION

In the end, if we do not have a pattern of observing Sabbath rest and recreation it is simply because we do not really believe it is a commandment; we do not believe the Word of God. We do not— to put it bluntly—trust ourselves or our work or our relationships to God. While the Sabbath for many has come to be defined as a day in which they do not work (and they call it a "day off"), it is important to stress that the prohibition against work was given for a reason: work would undermine the purpose of this special day, a day set aside for delight and joy in God and in God's creation.

The book of Genesis makes reference to the fact that at Creation God Himself rested after He did six days of creative work. Surely this is meant to call attention to the fact that the notion of Sabbath rest is not incidental or secondary to created life but rather something that is inherent in the Creation—and thus integral to a Christian spirituality.

Recreation is a discipline of the spiritual life that enables us to live in the world but not be of the world, to be a people that genuinely lives in light of the kingdom, in the underlying conviction that Jesus is Lord and that we live under His reign. When we observe Sabbath, we seek to live in truth. It is our nonverbal declaration that we trust God and place our hope in God. In a society consumed by work and commerce, it is imperative that we do everything we can to undermine the propensity to be fast paced. When we are consumed by work and activity and demands on our lives and our schedules, we are really only consumed with ourselves.

Having said this, we must also recognize and affirm that the character of a modern society and a modern city necessarily means that many cannot observe the Sabbath on Sunday. Ministers, police officers, hospital staff, and many others fulfill their God-given vocations in a way that naturally means they are occupied on Sunday. For these people, it is imperative that they find another day to observe as Sabbath. There are others who, because of their busyness in church or congregational life on a Sunday, might well choose to observe Sabbath rest on a Saturday or another day of the week. In other words, active involvement in church life may well be another form of work from which they need rest, Sabbath rest.

Some may wonder if there is a danger in speaking of recreation as a spiritual discipline — that we will return to the legalism of previous generations. While in our day we have become much too lax in our observance of seasons of rest and recreation, we are right to be cautious lest we create another inordinate burden for the people of God. The rule of thumb, though, is simple: the Sabbath is meant for joy — for the enjoyment of God, of life, of God's creation, and of the fellowship and encouragement we find in the people of God. We know something is wrong when the Sabbath no longer fosters joy.

This requires that we be disciplined — not overly scrupulous, perhaps, but certainly disciplined. Without discipline, there is no hope that this day will be saved and preserved and sustained as a special time in our week.

Recreation is the spiritual discipline of enjoying God's creation and God as Creator. For many if not most, worship will be an element or component of this discipline in their lives. But when we speak of recreation as spiritual discipline, we mean all those activities that are for us a foretaste of heaven. They are activities that declare in deed rather than word, you might say, that in the end all will be made well and that in God's timing, justice will come and peace will be established in our world.

Consequently, it follows that recreation begins with taking the creation seriously and enjoying it as the fruit of God's energies and work. In the Sabbath we have a day in which we no longer work to make things better, but step aside with friends and family to enjoy things as they are. We enjoy them because we enjoy life; we enjoy them in the context of all that God has made and that God Himself has declared to be good. For many, recreation will necessarily call them outdoors. Because they are in an office for their work week, Sabbath rest has to mean that they take intentional and purposeful joy in finding themselves on a hiking trail or in their garden.

For others, the spiritual discipline of recreation will mean that they develop a hobby. A hobby can be defined as any regular activity having no intrinsic worth in itself other than its affirmation of beauty and order. For individuals whose vocations place them under severe stress and frustration, a retreat into a hobby may well be one of the most essential elements that maintains sound mental health and hope in their calling. Engaging in a hobby becomes an act of faith—a regular, consistent means of declaring that beauty and order will prevail, although most of the evidence indicates otherwise. Through a hobby, whether stamp collecting, woodworking, or playing a musical instrument, we are further declaring that there is more to life than our work. We step back and delight in one aspect of the created order that has captured our imagination—some aspect of creation or culture that affirms beauty and order and fascinates us regardless of what others think of it.

For many, the spiritual discipline of recreation will include participation in music and the arts. More than any other dimension of culture, it is in music and the arts that the human person has the privilege of responding most fully as one who bears the image of God. Some would suggest that with discipline any person can learn to play a musical instrument and develop proficiency in one of the arts—be it painting, drama, or a handicraft.

For others, Sabbath rest is inconceivable without a good book, a book that is read not because it is useful or immediately helpful or because it is something that they *should* read; rather, it is the reading that is for nothing but the sheer joy of reading, of being lost in a narrative or mystery that is relished for no other reason than that it is a good story. And for others it will be poetry, both writing their own and reading the poems of others.

In leaving behind our occupations and labors in the world, we are freed to step into another world of fine music, literature, visual arts, handicrafts, and drama. We are freed to enjoy culture and to carry out the biblical mandate to have dominion over the earth and all that is in it. In a real sense, participation in music and the arts is a continual validation of the nature of our hope. We *live out* our hope; we do not merely work toward it. Our delight in friends, in a hobby, and in the arts is but one way of affirming, by faith, that the union of heaven and earth will consummate history and that ultimate reality lies in that consummation.

For yet others, recreation will necessarily mean vigorous physical activity, perhaps even a focused program of physical exercise. Again, depending on one's occupation, this may be the very best way by which one chooses to enjoy God's gift of life. Physical exercise can be an island of sanity in a bewildering and discouraging world; as such, it brings a foretaste of heaven.

However, regardless of how we observe Sabbath rest, the point is that this is as much a spiritual discipline as any: it is the intentional act of enjoying God's creation with friends and children. In this act we declare together that we do not save ourselves and that our hope rests in God and God alone. We are freed from our labors so that we can delight in God, in His creation, and in one another. It is an act whereby we affirm in faith that the kingdom has come but that it has not yet come in all its fullness.

Yet before I conclude this section on recreation, it is important also to mention that recreation is not an end in itself. Further, not all forms of recreation are inherently good. When our recreation dulls the mind—as do hours and hours of television—or when our play abuses the creation or our own bodies, or when recreation is but a subtle and misguided means by which we fuel selfishness or pride or our longing for power, something is clearly wrong. The Little League coach who spends all of his time shouting at his players is not celebrating anything other than his ego. Rather, recreation is only true when it is a spiritual discipline that fosters the good and the enjoyment of the good—when, in the language of Paul, we are drawn to and find joy in that which is good, noble, pure, and just (Philippians 4:8).

FRIENDSHIP

Recreation can be incorporated into our lives in various ways, and I have suggested some so far in this chapter. It can have both a private (such as pursuit of a hobby) as well as a communal dimension (such as play or participation in the arts). It may well be, however, that the most crucial way recreation is incorporated into a Christian spirituality is in the development of authentic friendships. True spirituality includes time with friends, an intimate association with our peers—time that is fun, enjoyable, and rewarding because of the sheer joy of human company.

True friendship is difficult to find, though. It does not take long to realize not only that true friends are rare, but also that false friends are present in abundance. There are those who are "friends" as long as they can get something from you. They are really seeking a customer; all they want is to sell you something. Sometimes you sense or know that this "friend" actually wants a financial contribution toward an organization. At other times, people want to ask for a favor or a contact so they can land a job. Selling a product in the context of a friendly conversation, soliciting an endorsement or funds for a worthy cause, or seeking help for a job are certainly not wrong in themselves. But they are wrong if those involved abuse the precious gift of friendship by acting as if or assuming that they are authentic friends. True friendship is rare.

Friendship is the foundational relationship of life. All other relationships are passing and temporal; friendships have the possibility of being eternal. Parent–child, teacher–student, pastor–parishioner, employer–employee are all passing relationships. These become lasting and eternal relationships when friendships develop — when a husband and wife are friends as well as spouses, when children mature to the point that they are friends with their parents and relate to them as brothers or sisters in Christ, when colleagues enjoy one another as persons and not merely as coworkers. C. S. Lewis stated it well: "Friendship seemed the happiest and most fully human of all loves, the crown of life and the school of virtue."[1] Friendships take time to develop and are not meant to be useful — in themselves. They are a foretaste of heaven; they are relationships in which people are enjoyed and appreciated merely because they are friends.

True spiritual maturity includes the development of friendships — relationships among men and women in whose company there is mutual acceptance, love, and encouragement. Without apology we need to recognize that in this life we will have few such friends. We may have many acquaintances, but the demands of intimate friendship are such that each individual will have few — possibly no more than three or four — at any given period of their lifetimes. Then, again without apology, we need to take time to be with friends for a meal together, an outing, or a time of conversation.

The point is that friendships will not happen naturally. They must be intentionally cultivated. This is due in part to the fact that, as James Olthius notes, friendship is the least necessary relation.[2] We have natural or instinctual commitments in marriage and family. We need to work and be part of a governed society. We need education. But we think we can get by without friends — intimate associations of mutual acceptance, reciprocity, and encouragement. Yet friendship is the foundational relationship of life. Without it, life is a wilderness and we miss out on the experience of one of God's most profound and life-sustaining gifts.

It would be helpful, perhaps, to indicate what it means to be a friend. Friendship is characterized, first, by equality. Friends are peers—people who freely choose to associate with one another. In friendship there is no superior, boss, or teacher. Some people do not know how to relate as a peer and therefore are immediately lost. Thus, learning to relate to people in a spirit of mutuality is part of learning to be a friend and to receive friendship.

Second, friends are drawn to each other by something they hold in common—common interests or concerns—that leads to camaraderie or what Olthius calls "congeniality."[3] Camaraderie could be centered on a common task or goal, a common concern or conviction, or some other mutual interest. But congeniality is more difficult to define. It is that unique something, that mysterious quality, that draws persons to each other, often with an apparent lack of common interests. There is a strange and unique bonding of personalities.

However, two individuals need not be peers or find each other particularly congenial for them to be friends. Friendship can cross cultural barriers, age differences, and many other apparent obstacles. The heart of friendship is commitment expressed in mutual acceptance, mutual appreciation, and mutual affirmation.

The black mark of friendship is treachery or broken trust; its hallmark, the demand for loyalty. By definition, this commitment leaves others out. It is a commitment that gives preference, special attention, and unique trust. True friends simply choose to support one another, depend on one another, and enjoy one another. As such, friends are perhaps the most tangible evidence of love other than that experienced in a healthy marriage. It is a gift from God—to be received with gratitude and cultivated carefully. Friendship is worth the investment of our time and energies.

What about cross-gender friendships? Paul exhorts Timothy to treat an older man as if he were his own father. Likewise, Timothy was to "treat younger men as brothers, older women as mothers, and younger women as sisters, with absolute purity" (1 Timothy 5:1-2, NIV). Timothy is given the freedom and encouragement to relate to women as his peers and friends, as though they were his sisters.

Of course, friendship often includes physical contact, but physical contact does not always indicate an erotic relationship—for instance, when a son embraces his mother. Friendships with the opposite sex need not threaten a marriage. In fact, friendships either with the same or the opposite sex can strengthen and support our marriages.

If a friendship leads to intense physical desire, however, then it must be ended. True friendship respects the commitments and associations we have made; a true sister respects her brother's marriage, and vice versa. If this trust is violated, the friendship will have to end. But this does not need to be the case. It *is* possible for men to treat women as sisters in all purity and for women to treat men as brothers in all purity.

The paramount example of such friendships is of Jesus Himself with two women very dear to him. Mary and Martha were special in His life. Very simply, the two women were His friends—sisters, whom he treated with purity.

Jesus told His disciples that He would no longer call them servants, but friends (John 15:15). He indicated that they had now entered into a unique relationship with Him, a relationship made for heaven. As followers of Jesus, we too have the privilege to call a fellow man or woman our friend. And when we do, we are going beyond the limits of our temporal, necessary, or natural relationships. We step into another time zone, another sphere of life. We have the power and the freedom to choose to give and receive friendship, to live in trust and commitment, and to enjoy reciprocal acceptance, appreciation, and affirmation.

Recreation is that element of our spirituality that will probably take the least of our time. But this does not make it less essential or less important. We need to make time (by saying "no" to the extended demands of our occupation and even sometimes of the church) and regularly find refreshment and quiet with our friends, our hobby, and the arts. Some individuals perhaps need to limit their leisure activities if this component has become their reason for living, to the neglect of the Christian community, their vocation, and the renewing of the mind. This imbalance, though, is not solved by the rejection of leisure or play. A well-rounded spirituality will include a routine—a rhythm of work, rest, play, and prayer. When the rhythm is disturbed, our spiritual lives suffer, whether the disruption occurs in our work or in our times of recreation.

◆ ◆ ◆ ◆ EPILOGUE

The genius of the spiritual life is that we sustain ever before us that, in response to the Spirit, we seek to know, love, and serve Jesus. We long to be in but not of the world—and in this genuine engagement to know complete joy.

And nothing matters more than our relationship with Jesus. This is the heart and soul of a genuine spirituality. On the one hand, this calls us to sustain the mystical side of our identity as Christians: nurturing a life of prayer, worship, and personal communion with Christ. We cannot be in but not of the world unless we are women and men of prayer.

But full identification with Christ also includes identifying with God's kingdom work in the world. Christ is establishing His kingdom of life and peace in this world. The earthly dimension of our spiritual life calls us to a full engagement with the world in response to God's call on our lives. Every element or component of a Christian spirituality has its vital place in our lives only because it is a means for us to live intentionally in personal relationship with Christ and in light of His kingdom. If we are able to live by the posture that we are in but not of the world, it is because we are intentional, conscious, and disciplined.

The first element—the renewal of our minds—enables us to know the truth and live by the truth. The apostle Paul makes it very clear that if we are not conformed to this world, it is because we are transformed by the renewal of our minds.

Second, we must also be in intentional relationship with Jesus through prayer. Without this connection, we will be lost and perplexed and rudderless in this world. Our only hope for abiding strength and joy is to find this very strength and joy in a personal encounter and relationship with Jesus.

The third element of the Christian life is vocation: being servants in the world, agents of God's truth and grace—the very means by which His kingdom purposes are accomplished in the church and in the world. To seek the kingdom does not mean that we long to escape the world; to the contrary, true spirituality calls us to an engagement in the world in the name of Jesus.

The fourth element—accountability and authority—is also imperative. We live in but not of the world when we live under the authority of Jesus. His authority finds concrete expression in our lives as we learn to live in accountability to one another.

And finally, when we practice the spiritual discipline of recreation, we proclaim that the reign of Jesus will one day be consummated. This world is broken, but one day all will be made well. And when we re-create, when we observe Sabbath rest, and when we know the joy of personal friendships, we live in anticipation of that day. Recreation is as vital a spiritual discipline as any.

In the end, though, each discipline is not an end in itself but a means to an end—that we would, in this broken and discouraging world, know the living water that is Jesus and drink deeply from the wellspring of God's grace.

A Suggested Format for Daily Prayer

The following is a suggested format that could be adapted to individual preferences or the needs of a particular day or prayer hour. It is important to find a place that is as secluded and quiet as possible, where you will be least likely to be interrupted or distracted.

Focus

Begin your prayers by an intentional act of being present to God. We so often come to our prayers distracted or emotionally pulled one way or the other. It makes sense, then, that in our prayers—just as in our daily physical exercise we are advised to do some warm-up exercises—we would begin with a simple act that would enable us to be mentally and emotionally present to God and to our own prayers.

What we need is a spiritual exercise that would enable us to center our thoughts on God; we long for minds that are stilled by the Spirit. One way to do this is to read a psalm or sing a hymn. I will sometimes stay with the same psalm for several days in a row. This way the psalm itself begins to take root in my conscience as I live and relive its call. I may stay with Psalm 23, for example, but a different phrase may capture and still my mind and heart one day, and then another phrase on another day. And I find it good to come to my prayers with a hymnbook and to consider a verse or the chorus to a well-known hymn. The value of a psalm or a hymn lies, in part, in the capacity of poetry to connect with us *both* intellectually and emotionally.

Obviously the whole of our time of prayer could be spent in this exercise, but I am envisioning only two or three minutes as we respond intentionally to Jesus as He calls us to prayer.

READING OF SCRIPTURE

Prayer is communion with God. He calls us to prayer and we respond by being present to Him. Now, with hearts and minds focused on Christ, we can attend to His Word. And thus a vital part of our daily prayers is the simple act of being present to a text of Holy Scripture through the exercise of meditation.

Read a text of Scripture—usually something of a length appropriate for the short time you have for your daily prayers, likely something you could read in three or four minutes. Read slowly, thoughtfully, and prayerfully. Recognizing the need to read the whole of their Bibles, some use their daily prayers to achieve this objective. They might follow worthy programs that call them to read through the whole Bible in a year, several chapters a day. However, while this is a worthwhile endeavor, what we so urgently need is reading that calls us deeper, reading that connects with the inner recesses of our hearts (Colossians 3:16). And for this we need to move slowly in our consideration of the text. Perhaps in another context you can take on the challenge of reading the whole Bible, but for our daily prayers, we need to read slowly, intentionally, and responsively.

But we do this in a way that honors the text as it was written. If the text is poetry (as are the Psalms), we read it and pray it as poetry. If we are in the letters of the New Testament, then we might consider a paragraph as the appropriate literary segment for our meditation. But though in meditation we take the text seriously, meditation is different from study. Study is the crucial exercise by which we ask, What did this text mean, particularly to the original hearers? What was the author intending to say and how might the text find application in our lives today? Meditation, in contrast, considers the question, Lord, what are you saying to me today through this ancient text, your Holy Word?

Ideally, then, the passage you consider in your meditation should be a text that is known to you, one in which you have already worked through and resolved some of the critical questions of interpretation (so that your prayers are not interrupted by perplexity about the original meaning of the text).

Consider a consecutive reading with each prayer time (for a week, perhaps) staying with the same text or moving on to the next passage within the same book of the Bible. You might spend two or more weeks in the book of Philippians, for example, praying one paragraph a day but moving on to the next paragraph only when you have an inner sense that it is good to do so. You are not racing through a text; rather, you are praying a text at a speed or rate that is congruent with your own inner response to God.

As you read and pray, allow the Word to settle more deeply in your consciousness; permit the Word to feed your soul and be a window to God and His purposes. Read, reread, and read again slowly. Contemplate Christ as revealed in Scripture (particularly if the text used is from the Gospels) and reflect on the implications of the Word for your life and work.

Consistently, you will find that God speaks through His ancient Word to the particularities of your life, work, and relationships. The text is ancient, but it has a remarkable relevance to every dimension of our lives.

Remember, though, that our daily prayers are a time of encounter and communion with Christ. We meditate on the text of Scripture that we would know, love, and serve Jesus. The text is not an end in itself; our daily prayers are not, in the end, a communion with the text, even though the text is the faithful and trustworthy Word of God. Rather, what we seek is Christ Himself as He is revealed and known through Scripture.

SILENCE

Then, in response to the text, be silent. God has spoken to us; the first response should certainly be silence. This may be difficult for some. But be still, if only for five minutes. Remember, words can get in the way of prayer if we are prone to wordiness. When the mind becomes distracted, gently but firmly turn back to an awareness of the presence of God.

RESPONSE

Then respond to what you sense God saying to you through Scripture with one (or more) of the following:

- ◆ *Adoration and praise.* Make a conscious, verbal affirmation of the goodness and glory of God, of the wonder of the creation, and of God's work of making all things well.

- ◆ *Thanksgiving.* Call to mind God's goodness and mercy, especially if in the silence you were conscious of a propensity to complain. Your response is an opportunity to consider the signs and indicators of God's goodness toward you and then to thank God again and again and again.

- ◆ *Confession.* Acknowledge failures and shortcomings before the Lord; seek and appropriate God's forgiveness. To confess is to respond in truth to the convicting ministry of the Spirit, who calls us from death to life.

- ◆ *Care-casting.* Identify your fears and worries, and cast these cares upon your heavenly Father.

Each of these four—adoration, thanksgiving, confession, and care-casting—could be part of your daily prayers *every* day, but one or the other will be more appropriate at different times. As appropriate, these four exercises might also be a means to focus your thoughts at the beginning of your prayer.

DISCERNMENT

As we look back over the past day and then ahead to the day before us, our prayer is also an opportunity to consider the particular word of God to us for that day—whether it be encouragement, wisdom in the face of a decision or a choice, or counsel in the face of a difficult meeting that lies ahead—when we know we need to listen well and speak well.

Reflect on the joys and sorrows of the past day; identify where the Lord is seeking to make an impression on your conscience. Note particularly the thoughts that arose during the time of silence following the meditation on Scripture. In this regard, place before the Lord the duties and responsibilities that lie before you and consider what activities most reflect God's call to you that day.

INTERCESSION

Pray that God's will would be done on earth; pray for colleagues, family, friends, and others (including those who oppose you or make life and work difficult for you), that they would know the grace, wisdom, and strength of God. Reflect on the challenges, problems, and opportunities you face and ask for divine assistance. He is ready to help in our time of need. I find it helpful to work with a regular list of those for whom I pray, with a different list and focus for each day. But this is only one way to approach our ministry of intercession for others. Do what seems right for you as you serve family, friends, colleagues, and others by asking for the intervention of God's grace in their lives.

RENEWED COMMITMENT

Finally, it is good to conclude our daily prayers with a renewed resolve to live according to the purposes of God in obedience to His Word and by His grace. With open heart and mind, we can with confidence now leave our prayers and embrace the work we have been given, but we do so as women and men who have chosen to know, love, and serve Jesus. If there has been a word of direction or guidance discerned during the time of prayer, we now respond with a willingness to do God's will, to live by His grace under His Word.

Then, in conclusion, why not return to the psalm or the hymn with which you began your prayers? Where you began is often a good place to conclude.

♦ ♦ ♦ ♦ 2

A Suggested Format
for a Day of Prayer

In some respects a day of prayer is merely an extension and expansion of our daily prayers. But with more time we can respond more deliberately to the presence of God and His Word. It is helpful to approach a day of prayer or a spiritual retreat well prepared. Have a plan. It is also good to set a purpose from the beginning. Will your retreat be an extended prayer time with God, or are you seeking a word of direction or guidance from the Lord? Bring the following resources for the retreat.

♦ A Bible in a contemporary translation

♦ A good hymnbook with an extended section of classic hymns of praise and adoration

♦ An unused notebook to serve as a journal

♦ Perhaps a devotional classic (see Appendix 4), especially if you anticipate a more extended time of prayer (such as a weekend)

One way to approach a day of prayer is to divide the day into four parts, each of which is composed of one extended ninety-minute time of focused prayer, or if you prefer, two periods of forty to forty-five minutes. For each period, consider following the basic format of the daily prayer as suggested in Appendix 1: a time in which you focus attention and seek to be present to the Lord (using a psalm or a hymn, perhaps the same psalm throughout the day), meditation on Scripture, silence, and response. The response would generally correspond to the grace sought in that period of the day, as suggested by the outline below. You might then save the renewal of commitment until the fourth segment of your prayer and the conclusion of the day.

You might conclude each prayer period with a few comments in your journal describing your impressions, addressing God and telling Him what is happening in prayer and what you hear Him saying.

The following order is adapted from St. Ignatius Loyola's *Spiritual Exercises*.

Part 1: Thanksgiving and Remembrance

For this first segment to the day, the grace we seek is the assurance that God loves us. And we seek this grace through the spiritual disciplines of thanksgiving. After reading appropriate Scripture, reflect on it and list the evidences of God's goodness in your life. Recall the circumstances of your conversion and your call to ministry or to the vocation through which you serve God. Enumerate God's blessings to you from both the distant past as well as in the immediate circumstances of your life and work.
Suggested Scriptures: Psalms 28, 63, and 84; Romans 8:28-39

Part 2: Knowing Yourself

For the second segment of the day, the grace we seek is to see ourselves as God sees us. To this end, it is good to come with open heart and mind to the prayer of confession: in humility we ask God to give us greater insight into our character and the pattern of our thought, speech, and behavior. Be honest and open; nothing is gained by hiding the truth or making excuses for what is true; we want to see ourselves as God sees us. Reflect on the joys and sorrows of recent days and weeks; seek evidence of the

Spirit's work in your life and His call to growth and maturity. Enumerate these, confessing sin and shortcomings, acknowledging God's grace where there has been strength, perseverance, and joy. Identify your fears and worries and cast your cares on your heavenly Father.

Suggested Scriptures: Psalm 139:23-24; Matthew 5–7; Ephesians 4:17–5:21; Colossians 3

Part 3: Knowing Christ

For this segment of the day of prayer, the grace we seek is to know Christ so that we love Him more deeply and serve Him more eagerly and effectively. To this end we seek Christ as revealed and known through Scripture. Read with this in mind: open your heart and mind as Christ is revealed to you. Ask as you read that you would come to a more intimate and personal knowledge of His love, His character, and His mission (the nature of His work in the world).

If you have come to this day of prayer seeking guidance for a particular issue or decision in your life, it is very possible that the mind of Christ will come clear to you during this segment of the day.

Suggested Scriptures: John 6:1-14,16-24; 11:17-44; Philippians 2:1-11; Hebrews 4:14-16

Part 4: Following Christ

Now we seek the grace to take up our cross and follow Christ as His disciples. Hear again the Word of Christ to be His disciple and servant; reflect on the unique circumstances of that call in response to what has been impressed upon your heart and mind through the course of the day of prayer. Make a fresh commitment to be faithful to that call and to your identity in Christ.

Suggested Scriptures: John 13:1-17; 15:7-17; 2 Corinthians 5:16–6:2; Philippians 3:7–4:1

DISCOVERING
YOUR VOCATION

Recognizing one's vocation is as much a process of self-discovery as of discerning God's will. God's call is not arbitrary; it reflects our *dreams* and our *abilities*. Consequently, part of vocational discovery arises from self-knowledge.

In chapter 12 of Paul's letter to the Romans, the apostle enumerates seven gifts by which men and women contribute to the life of the church and to the world. It has been suggested that these are best understood as motivational gifts, as contributions we make that reflect our deep desires and our God-given abilities. The seven gifts are (1) prophesying, (2) serving, (3) teaching, (4) encouraging, (5) contributing to the needs of others, (6) leadership, and (7) showing mercy. If these are motivational gifts, then it is fair to conclude that each person will have only one or a dominant motivation and will function best when he or she does so in terms of this gift or call. Therefore, part of self-discovery is a recognition of this motivational gift.

Various forms and tests have been designed to help Christians discover their motivational gift, but I have found it helpful to think in terms of a potential ministry setting. Imagine you have entered into the emergency ward of a hospital and discovered that the patients are lying everywhere, the lone nurse is off to the side enjoying a cigarette, there are no doctors in sight, the walls are unpainted, and the wounded are weeping in pain. What do you do? My suggestion is that people will respond in seven classic ways that correspond to the seven motivational gifts.

One will recognize immediately that the problem is that the doctors and nurses will not fulfill their responsibilities. They know what is right and they have the means to fulfill their duties, but they need someone to call them to accountability. This person sees his role as that of calling people to an encounter with the truth. His gift or contribution is *prophesying*.

Others have heard enough preaching and teaching and feel the need of the hour is action, for women and men who will get involved with their hands and energies. They are hands-on people, and they see what needs to be done and get out and do it. They have the gift of *service*.

Another sees the main problem to be one wherein the nurses and doctors do not understand their responsibilities; what is needed is careful explanation. This person is convinced that things will be better when people understand the truth. Her contribution is that of *teaching*.

Still others look at the situation as one lacking hope. To them, what is needed is a restoration of that hope. They suspect that the hospital is so run-down because the staff is discouraged, so these people bring *encouragement*. Some are encouragers through their words; others encourage by providing environments of beauty and peace that sustain hope and courage.

Another might look at the situation and decide immediately that what is needed is funding. This person is inclined to think, *Nothing can be accomplished without money, and I know how to raise it.* He is not cold-hearted; its merely that his gift is that of *contributing to the needs of others*.

Yet another might look at the situation and recognize at once that the main problem is organization. What is needed is a person to serve as a catalyst and provide quality *administration* — to recruit doctors and nurses and assure that the proper equipment and supplies are available so they can do their work. A leader is effective to the extent that she governs diligently as a servant, freeing others to perform their ministries.

Finally, Paul identifies a seventh contribution. The encourager focuses on the doctors and the nurses. The one who serves immediately gets about the task of tending to the wounded. But there is another whose principal contribution is that of going to the wounded and holding them, carrying their burdens and pains with them. This person shows *mercy* and does so with cheer.

Which of the seven is most important? None. If we look closely we soon see that all seven are a composite picture of the Messiah, our Lord Jesus. He is all seven of these to the church and the world, and He works through us to fulfill His ministry as each of us exercises his or her motivational gift.

Recognizing our gift does not answer immediately the vocational question, but it is the first step in reflecting on where we can make our best contribution. It can help us make a sober-minded choice when two options are before us and one of them is clearly not a reflection of our dreams and abilities.

DEVOTIONAL CLASSICS FOR SPIRITUAL READING

Recommended for All Readers

Thomas à Kempis, *The Imitation of Christ*
St. Augustine, *Confessions*
Dietrich Bonhoeffer, *Life Together* and *The Cost of Discipleship*
Richard Foster, *The Celebration of Discipline*
Thomas Merton, *New Seeds of Contemplation*
A. W. Tozer, *The Pursuit of God*
Dallas Willard, *The Divine Conspiracy*

Also Worth Reading

John Donne, *Devotions*
St. Francis de Sales, *On the Love of God*
Gustavo Gutierrez, *On Job*
St. Ignatius of Loyola, *Spiritual Exercises*
St. John of the Cross, *Ascent of Mt. Carmel* and *Dark Night of the Soul*
Thomas Kelly, *A Testament of Devotion*
William Law, *A Serious Call to a Devout and Holy Life*
Blaise Pascal, *Pensées*
St. Teresa of Avila, *Interior Castle*

This is not an exhaustive list. It is selective of different traditions and styles—a place to begin. The works listed under "Also Worth Reading" may require more patience, care, and discernment in order to appreciate their messages.

Reading devotional classics requires an approach that is different from other kinds of reading we do. Here are some suggestions.

◆ Read at a time of the day when you are mentally alert.

◆ Find a time each week, possibly Sunday afternoon after a siesta, to read for an hour or two.

◆ Refuse to read anything just once; read each paragraph or section at least twice, if not more often.

◆ Use a pencil and mark where you have questions unresolved. Note where you concur and find encouragement from the author and also where you are troubled or challenged (you may wish to use a code system to mark the text).

◆ Conclude with some annotations in a journal or notebook, identifying what you are learning and where the Lord is calling for growth.

♦ ♦ ♦ ♦ NOTES

CHAPTER 1: A Spirituality That Fits

1. A. W. Tozer, *The Pursuit of God* (Harrisburg, PA: Christian Publications, 1948), p. 17.
2. Tozer, p. 67.
3. Joseph de Guibert, *The Spiritual Doctrine of Jesus*, trans. William J. Young, ed. George E. Ganss (Chicago: Institute of Jesuit Sources, 1964) pp. 8-9.
4. Guibert, pp. 8-9.

CHAPTER 2: The Renewal of the Mind

1. *The Confessions of St. Augustine*, bk. 10, trans. John K. Ryan (New York: Image, 1960), chap. 8, para. 15.
2. See Armando Valladares, *Against All Hope*, trans. Andrew Hurley (New York: Knopf, 1987).
3. Kosuke Koyama, *Three Mile an Hour God* (Maryknoll, NY: Orbis, 1979), p. 54.
4. Jeanne Cover, "Theological Reflections: Social Effects of Television," *Religious Education* 78 (Winter 1983), pp. 38-49.
5. See Neil Postman, *The Disappearance of Childhood* (New York: Seabury Press, 1982).
6. See Dag Hammarskjöld, *Markings*, trans. Leif Sjoberg and W. H. Auden (New York: Knopf, 1963), p. 147.
7. See Thomas Merton, *New Seeds of Contemplation* (London: Burns and Oates, 1961), p. 140.

CHAPTER 3: Personal Encounter with God

1. Presented in lectures on the history of spirituality in July 1982 at Regent College, Vancouver, Canada.

2. This three-fold paradigm is an adaptation from the classic spiritual ideal of the Middle Ages: knowing, loving, and following Jesus.
3. Quoted in John Carmody, *Reexamining Conscience* (New York: Seabury Press, 1982), p. 30.
4. The term "care-casting" was suggested to me through a sermon delivered by Rev. David Moore in Nyack, New York, in August 1987.
5. For a more complete study of discernment, decision making, and divine guidance, consider my full-length study of this subject, *Listening to God in Times of Choice* (Downers Grove, IL: InterVarsity, 1997).

CHAPTER 4: Vocation and Christian Service

1. Dietrich Bonhoeffer, *Life Together* (New York: Harper & Row, 1954), pp. 69-70.
2. A. W. Tozer, *The Pursuit of God*, (Harrisburg, PA: Christian Publications, 1948), p. 123.
3. See James W. Fowler, *Becoming Adult, Becoming Christian: Adult Development and Christian Faith* (San Francisco: Harper & Row, 1984).
4. Fowler, p. 95.
5. See Fowler, pp. 103-104.
6. Fowler, p. 126.
7. For a more comprehensive examination of a Christian understanding of vocation, see my publication *Courage and Calling: Embracing Your God-Given Potential* (Downers Grove, IL: InterVarsity, 1999).

CHAPTER 5: Spiritual Authority and Accountability

1. David Augsburger, "The Private Lives of Public Leaders," *Christianity Today* 31 (Nov. 20, 1987), pp. 23-24.
2. Alan Jones, *Exploring Spiritual Direction: An Essay on Christian Friendship* (San Francisco: Harper & Row, 1982), p. 3.

3. Thomas H. Green, S. J., *Come Down Zacchaeus* (Notre Dame: Ave Maria Press, 1987), p. 95.

4. Jones, p. 19.

CHAPTER 6: Recreation

1. Quoted in James Olthius, *I Pledge You My Troth* (San Francisco, Harper & Row, 1975), p. 107.

2. Olthius, p. 108.

3. Olthius, p. 110.

GORDON T. SMITH is the academic vice president and dean of Regent College in Vancouver, British Columbia, where he also has a teaching appointment in spiritual theology. He is an ordained minister with the Christian and Missionary Alliance, and has pastored both in Canada and the Philippines. Gordon is the author of several books including *Listening to God in Times of Choice* and *Courage and Calling* (both IVP). His personal vision is to enable Christians to think theologically about all of life. Gordon lives in Vancouver with his wife, Joella.